Basingstoke is a phenomenon. One of the  in England it is
renowned for its pointless roundabouts, v                                    le
Modernist architecture, and treated as a joke
widely recognised for its contribu

C000205514

Using all his ingenuity, Rupert Willoughby ha                                    is
mission to rehabilitate Basingstoke. He descɪɪᴠᴇᴇ .                                   d
post-war planners wilfully robbed the town of its individuality and charm. Yet a
nobler Basingstoke lies buried under the concrete - the Basingstoke of Walter de
Merton, the medieval pioneer of university education; of Jane Austen, who attended
regular balls in the old Town Hall and describes them in her novels; of Thomas
Burberry, inventor of the raincoat and reformer of dress, whose influence on
fashion is felt to this day; and of Margaret Chandler, who has lent her name to a
delightfully sunny spot in Australia.

This is local history with a difference. Imbued with a strong sense of place, it is
accurate but rarely impartial. The author strives to be anything but dry and
reverential, yet evokes with great sympathy the tragi-comic lives of Basingstoke's
former inhabitants. He cannot make you like the town, but at the end you may, at
least, understand it.

COLLEGIVM MERTONENSE,

VIEW BY BEREBLOCK, 1566. [*Facsimile from Hearne.*]

# BASINGSTOKE
# AND ITS
# CONTRIBUTION
# TO WORLD
# CULTURE

*Rupert Willoughby*

Designed by Catherine Roberts
and published by the author at
1 Railway Terrace, Stratfield Mortimer,
Reading, Berks., RG7 3PA

www.rupertwilloughby.co.uk

Printed by Creeds the Printers,
Broadoak, Bridport, Dorset, DT6 5NL

ISBN 978 0 9534428 6 7

*Frontispiece.* A view across the churchyard of Queen Anne House, with (below) the same view today. A building of considerable architectural and historical interest, it was demolished in 1967. Some would question whether the 'Great Wall of Basingstoke' was an acceptable substitute.

*Endpiece.* Basingstoke in 2010. A brave new world?

*Back cover illustration* © *R. Applin.* Robert Cottle's view of the Market Place, Basingstoke, dated 1831. The elegant Town Hall, built in 1657, was soon to be demolished: it was thought to intrude into the square. Jane Austen, who attended regular balls in its grand Assembly Rooms, once dancing twenty dances in an evening 'without any fatigue', would surely have mourned its loss. The buildings on the right of the picture had to make way for the new Town Hall. Basingstoke's days as a busy coaching town were also numbered: the railways were to arrive in 1839.

TO MY MOTHER

and to the memory
of her great-grand-aunt,
Margaret Chandler
of Basingstoke

# Contents

'Arrivata l'A.S. per tempo a Busenstoke fece un giro a piede per il luogo, infelice e per l'abitazioni, che sono la maggior parte di legno, e per la mancanza del negozio, onde la soddisfazione della curiosità non arrivò a pagare la fatica di pochi passi.'

Lorenzo Magalotti, 1669

'What goes for Basingstoke goes for most English country towns.'

Sir John Betjeman

'Practically all the centre of the town was demolished and re-developed in a coarse and brutal manner in the 1960s and, since then, there have been added on the outskirts tower-blocks of offices surrounded by tangled knots of motorway roundabouts, the whole now creating a huge and incongruous urban blot on the Hampshire landscape.'

Deirdre Le Faye

'Nothing can happen here, nothing has ever happened here, the 20th century was a bad dream.'

Owen Hatherley

# Introduction

Basingstoke is one of the most derided towns in England. Its reputation is as an over-developed eyesore of numbing dullness. Its very name lends itself to mockery. Basingrad, Basingjoke, Blazingsmoke, Boringstoke and even the ironic Amazingstoke are variants thought up and used by its own residents, not always with affection.

Though it is best known for its bewildering succession of pointless roundabouts, the curse of the town is its ridiculous, often hostile 'Modernist' architecture, much of it illustrated and described on Joe Tozer's witty website ('It's Basingstoke not Boringstoke'). The most notorious feature is the so-called 'Great Wall of Basingstoke', a huge retaining wall, built in the 1960s, for 'the great mass of concrete poured over the razed remains of the old market town'. Also of note are the 'Hanging Gardens of Basingstoke', a misfired attempt at horticulture on the top of a 1970s steel-and-glass block, and the 'Costa del Basingstoke', a gaily-coloured apartment complex in the style of a 'Costa' resort ('however as Basingstoke has no beach it has to make do with a view over the town's enormous car park'). The town's most risible attraction is surely the prominent sculpture that locals have dubbed the 'Wote Street Willy'. Said to be an image of a mother and child, it is actually 'the largest phallus on public display in Britain'. One thinks also of the 'Toy Town' tower that looms over Festival Place, and wonders if it, too, is a phallic reference. A town that treats itself as a joke can hardly expect to be taken seriously by outsiders.

In my most recent book, the whimsically-entitled *Reading and its Contribution to World Culture*, I set out to examine whether the town on the Thames was truly the 'desolate, unenlightened place' that it at first appeared. I discovered its associations over the centuries with a number of prominent writers and poets and was reassured that some of them had found inspiration in the town. Basingstoke is a phenomenon that, even more than Reading, cries out for a similar evaluation. What is the intelligent person to make of it? What has he ever made of it? This book is a light-hearted attempt to fill that gap and answer those questions.

Unfortunately, though almost every significant figure in English history must at some time have passed through Basingstoke (owing to its position on the Great Western Road), its appeal to poets and writers has been limited. Jane Austen, who lived locally, never had a good word to say of it. The Wartons (father and son) were rare exceptions but are relatively minor poets. Gilbert White, who was old Warton's pupil at the Vicarage, joined a local gang that amused itself by vandalising the Holy Ghost Chapel, as he shamefacedly admits in his *Natural History and Antiquities of Selborne*. The outstanding resident poet was Thomas Hardy, who lodged at Dinmont House (not yet identified) for a few weeks in the summer of 1897, during celebrations for the Queen's Jubilee. Basingstoke was ideal as a 'temporary base', being 'only about an hour from Town' and, one suspects, the sort of undemanding, provincial setting in which he (and Mrs Hardy) felt most comfortable.

Was Hardy aware that the very name 'teems with hidden meaning'? The mere mention of it induced hilarity among the contemporary audiences of *Ruddigore*. The development of the town since the 1960s has robbed it of almost every vestige of its former charm, yet it has probably always seemed a dull, shabby, uninspiring sort of place. On 13 April 1669, Cosimo III de' Medici, Grand Duke of Tuscany, paused here on a journey from Plymouth to London, spending the night probably at the Angel or the Maidenhead. His secretary, Count Lorenzo Magalotti, describes how 'His Highness, arriving betimes at Basingstoke, set out to explore it on foot, but it seemed so wretched, being full of wooden houses and empty of trade, that the gratification of his curiosity hardly repaid the effort of walking a few paces.' Admittedly, the Duke was used to the Florentine Duomo and the Palazzo della Signoria, but even St Michael's Church was a disappointment - 'a small and very indifferent building'. It was churlish of the Duke, while inspecting it, to decline the offer of the Mayor and two other officers to pay their formal respects. He was a pompous young fellow who had long since given up smiling in public. At least he commissioned his artist to sketch the town from the Liten, St Michael's standing out among the thatched roofs. The earliest surviving image of Basingstoke, it is reproduced in the town's Willis Museum, though without the accompanying description.

Untrammelled by the requirement to present a reverential, expurgated or 'official' version, I aim in this book to probe beneath the surface of Basingstoke. It has had its moments of excitement, and is in many ways a typical English town. I cannot make you like it, but at the end you may, at least, understand it.

Kind friends have been extraordinarily generous with their time and expertise. I am particularly grateful to Bob and Barbara Applin, John Hollands, John Alferink and Jan Matthews of the Margaret River District Historical Society, Pat Murphy, Joe Tozer, David Selwyn, Deirdre Le Faye, Peter Whicher and Edmund Cookson. Thanks also to Kim Oakley for the kind loan of her scarf, and to Rosie, my muse, for nursing me through a very severe case of writer's block.

# I. The Raincoat Revolution

**B**asingstoke's greatest contribution to world culture has, arguably, been the invention of the raincoat. It is largely forgotten that the world-famous Burberry brand, which has so transformed outdoor fashion that one can hardly conceive of life without it, originated in Basingstoke.

The Victorian founder of the firm, the enterprising Thomas Burberry, kept a draper's shop at 20 Winchester Street. He was a farmer's son, born at Brockham Green, near Dorking, on 27 August 1835, and had served his apprenticeship with a country draper. In 1856, when barely of age, he had acquired the premises for his new shop at a particularly strategic location in Basingstoke, then an important crossroads and a thriving market town.

Burberry understood the needs of the farmer, horseman, fisherman and shooting man, being all of these himself. He became a specialist in outdoor wear, and his emporium was much frequented by the local farmers and sportsmen. In 1868 he opened a small factory in New Street for the production of his own garments. Keen to develop an improved outer garment, one that would be as cool in summer as it was warm in winter, he approached his doctor for advice. Was it healthier to wear a coat that, in heavy rain, allowed one to become 'wet through', or should one always be kept dry inside, even if the garment itself became clammy and saturated? Burberry's doctor (never identified, unfortunately - and there was stiff competition in Basingstoke at the time) favoured the garment that was resistant to wind and rain, though he stressed the importance of 'natural ventilation'.

It occurred to Burberry that the loose-fitting peasants' smocks that were widely worn by country people seemed to have all the required characteristics, being wind and water resistant and comfortable in all weathers. He noted the close weave of the fabric on these smocks, and how it was surface tension that prevented the penetration of water. Peasants who had contact with sheep seemed to acquire additional protection through the oily lanolin in the wool. Finally, the loose style of these smocks ensured that they were well ventilated.

With the help of a cotton mill owner, Burberry set about improving on this material. The long staple Egyptian cotton which he used was, by some secret process, doubly proofed - first in the yarn, before weaving, and then again in the piece. Within a few years he had developed an untearable cloth which, whilst waterproof, was also cool and breathable, and called it 'gabardine'.

In 1879 Burberry registered his untearable cloth as a trade mark. The name 'gabardine' was not new, though it is difficult to know whether it was in widespread use or where Burberry might have heard it. Apparently it was another name for the peasant smock, from the Old French *gauvardine,* which occurs in 1520. Ultimately it may derive from the Middle High German *wallevart* meaning 'pilgrimage', for the same sort of long, loose, woven smock had traditionally been the uniform of the pilgrims who had been such a common sight on medieval roads, along with their staff and scrip.

Burberry is undoubtedly to be credited with having popularised the word, which in due course became a generic term for all designs of waterproof fabric, not only those emanating from Basingstoke. In 1888 his 'materials for garments for sportsmen' were patented for the first time. In 1889, ten years after launching his 'gabardine', Burberry expanded his business to London. He traded at first from rooms in the Jermyn Street Hotel, and in 1891 licensed one of his employees, R.B. Rolls, to trade under his name at 30 Haymarket. Burberry had by now been joined in the business by his sons Thomas Newman and Alfred Michael. Rolls, who had previously worked for them at Basingstoke, became a partner in Thomas Burberry and Sons in 1901.

Burberry's had been purveyors not only of clothing and fabrics but also, from a shop on Church Street, of china, furniture and ironmongery. The firm's most marketable product was, however, the new 'gabardine' raincoat. Known as 'the slip-on', it was available in five weights - 'Airylight', 'Double-Weave', 'Karoo', 'Wait-a-Bit' and 'Tropical'. Burberry personally supervised production from a new shop and offices that he had opened in London Street in 1892, with an expanded factory at the rear, bounded by Mark Lane and Hackwood Road.

Burberry sold the original factory in New Street to John Mares, a former partner, who himself became a manufacturer of raincoats under the 'Peltinvain' label. Another former partner, William Gerrish, who in 1878 bought the ready-made part of the business, founded the firm of Gerrish, Ames and Simpkins, clothing manufacturers, on Station Hill, on what is now the site of the 'Malls'. Finally, in August 1914, Burberry sold the Winchester Street store (rebuilt after a disastrous fire in 1905) to Edgar Lanham, who, like Rolls, Mares and Gerrish, had been a trusted colleague. Thomas Burberry had thus spawned an entire clothing industry that, in the first half of the 20$^{th}$ century, was one of the main employers in Basingstoke.

Now that others had taken up his idea, Burberry had his 'gabardine' material patented in 1900. The finished products were sent up to London, to a warehouse in Golden Square, whence, from the early 1900s, they were distributed to his shop on the Haymarket and to branches in Paris, New York, Buenos Aires and Montevideo. The Basingstoke factory employed 300 hands by 1920 and the firm boasted no fewer than 22,000 agents both at home and abroad. The London headquarters were moved in 1912 to 18-22 Haymarket, whence Burberry's continued to trade until 2009, when the firm relocated to the open-plan, concrete and glass Horseferry House in Westminster.

It is difficult to appreciate the novelty of a garment that is now taken for granted, but Burberry was, no less than Beau Brummel, a reformer of dress. People wondered how they had ever managed without 'raincoats'. Charles Macintosh had famously patented his rubberised waterproof coats in 1823, but these sticky, smelly, easily punctured garments, which were apt to melt in hot weather and to stiffen in cold, were a crude concept when compared with Burberry's silky gabardine. In the nineteenth century, no person of fashion would dream of wearing a 'Mac'.

Burberry also supplied a variety of weatherproofs to the army, including the 'Great-Coat' (double-breasted, half-belted, fur-lined), the 'British Warm' (short, straight, double-breasted), the 'Cavalry Waterproof' (knee-length, flared with back vent) and the 'Infantry Pattern' (knee-length, wide, with centre buttoning). Burberry's pattern for an officer's raincoat was personally approved by Edward VII in 1902. The most fashionably-dressed man in the world wore one himself and his habit of calling for his 'Burberry' ensured that the name became synonymous with 'raincoat', rather as one refers to vacuum cleaners, of whatever make, as 'Hoovers'. Some of these styles are worn by army officers to this day and indeed the author occasionally sports a fine vintage specimen of a 'British Warm' which he inherited from his father, who had it run up in the 1950s by his own military tailor in Hong Kong.

Burberry's design for an army officer's raincoat, known as the 'Trench Coat', was the regulation style during the Great War, the Basingstoke factory supplying half a million of them to the armed forces. Fitted with epaulettes, straps and D-strings, it was adapted in one version, the 'Trench Warm', by the addition of an inner cashmere layer to provide three coats in one, no doubt much appreciated by officers who were damp and freezing in the trenches of the Western Front. Lest the senior service should feel left out, there was also the 'Naval Burberry' in an appropriate colour.

Ever adaptable, Burberry and Sons had been quick, in the early 1900s, to produce specialist clothing for devotees of the motoring craze, who included the King. Clouds of dust were thrown up by the early open-topped cars as they roared along the neglected highways. Burberry clad the exposed motorists in double-breasted tweed and leatherwear which could be buttoned up to the chin and, at the same time, wrapped around the legs in the manner of a travelling rug. The 'enormous overcoat' in which Mr Toad is attired for motoring in Kenneth Grahame's *Wind in the Willows,* as illustrated by E.H. Shepard, is surely a 'Burberry'. The styles for motorists included the evocatively-named 'Viator', 'Rusitor', 'Auto Weather-All' and 'Burberry Dust Wrappers'.

Others with pioneering spirit, from explorers and big game hunters to balloonists and aviators, could expect to be individually catered for by Burberry. The foremost Arctic explorers, Amundsen, Scott and Shackleton, each wore Burberry gabardine windproof overalls on their expeditions. When Scott arrived at the South Pole in 1912, it was to find the Burberry gabardine tent that his Norwegian rival, Amundsen, had pitched there. Amundsen later dispatched a highly complimentary letter to Basingstoke:

> *'Dear Sirs, Heartiest thanks, Burberry overalls were made extensive use of during the sledge journey to the Pole and proved real good friends indeed.'*

For his part, Shackleton popularised the 'Shackleton Outrig Suit', a gabardine suit of the utmost simplicity, with only a drawstring to secure it. The members of his 1914 trans-Antarctic expedition, which turned out to be one of the greatest adventures of all time, were all kitted out in homely gabardine clothing that had been made up for them by the senior tailoresses at Basingstoke.

Similarly, the early aviator Claude Grahame-White, founder in 1911 of the Hendon Aerodrome, dressed himself in a Burberry gabardine 'Aeroplane Outrig', and Burberry kit was worn by Captain Sir John Alcock and Lieutenant Arthur Brown who, in 1919, were the first men to fly across the Atlantic. Burberry treasured a personal letter that he received from Alcock:

> *'I am writing to tell you how very satisfactory the outfit proved which I ordered from you for the Atlantic flight.*
>
> *Although in a continual mist, rain or sleet, and the altitude varying from 200 to 11,000 feet causing great variations in temperature, I kept as dry, warm and comfortable as it is possible to be under such conditions.*
>
> *This is a wonderful achievement for Burberry's, especially considering that I never adopted any electrical or other artificial means of heating, and that no rubber or cement is used in your waterproofing.'*

With Alcock's fulsome recommendation behind him, Burberry's designs, including the 'Air Warm', were naturally taken up by the newly-formed R.A.F. in 1923, but the firm - a limited company since 1920 - continued to cater for enthusiasts of a wide variety of leisure pursuits, including golf, archery, tennis, bicycling, skiing, skating and motorcycling. For example, the 1924 Everest Expedition, on which Mallory and Irvine perished, probably after reaching the summit, was equipped with gabardine. The peak of Everest, the South Pole, the skies above the Atlantic - each was conquered with the help of Burberry of Basingstoke, whose name had become famous throughout the civilised world.

Thomas Burberry was a characteristic Victorian entrepreneur. Inventive, industrious, scrupulously honest and fair, benevolent and patriarchal, he was also, like many of that type, a Nonconformist. Enjoying 'a vigorous constitution' into his eighties, Burberry 'was a total abstainer from intoxicating liquors, a non smoker, and followed a rule of life which by most people would be regarded as singularly frugal'. For many years he lived over the shop in Winchester Street. By the 1870s, having converted the flat into accommodation for his female staff, he resided at 'The Mount', a Georgian house on Bounty Road. In the early 1900s he moved to Crossways in Hook (formerly known as Viney's Folly), whence, though well over seventy, he would ride into Basingstoke on horseback, until a fall into a ditch encouraged him to find alternative means of transport.[1]

Soon after moving to Hook, then a small settlement on the main highway, Burberry provided it with a fully-furnished social club and meeting room. He claimed at its opening in October 1912 that he had 'learnt two things at his mother's knee - the first was to love God and His Book; the second was to love his neighbour and seek to do him good'. Burberry was a 'Strict and Particular Baptist' - a pared-down version of the ordinary Baptist - and had helped in 1867 to build the Ebenezer Chapel on Church Street, where he was a regular worshipper. He would often ride out as far as Whitchurch

[1] Burberry's son, Thomas Newman, had lived since 1909 in considerably grander style at 'The Shrubbery' in Cliddesden Road, surrounded by a private golf-course, tennis courts and cricket pitches, and attended by a large staff including a butler and a chauffeur clad in a brown Burberry uniform.

in order to preach to his fellow sectarians. Particular Baptists know themselves to be unworthy sinners who have been shown unmerited grace, so it is incumbent on them actively to consider the welfare of other Christians. Thus Burberry put up a sign by the side door at Crossways, assuring passing tramps that they would be fed and made welcome. Once a month in winter, he would preside over inter-denominational meetings in Basingstoke Town Hall, which were piously billed as being 'for the deepening of Spiritual life'.

In his youth Burberry had been a leading figure in the Total Abstinence Society, often chairing its meetings at Basingstoke. It is necessary to appreciate that drunkenness was at that time a terrible affliction on the town. Burberry part-owned the Basingstoke Mineral Water Company, which operated from premises in Church Street (behind what is now a computer cartridge shop), and was a director of the company which converted the Old Angel Inn, on the south-west corner of the Market Place, into a 'temperance café'. Burberry further served the town as Vice-President of the Basingstoke branch of the National Deposit Friendly Society and in 1881 stood for election to the town council, losing out by a matter of a few votes. According to his obituary, 'the election was made memorable by a serious riot accompanied by destruction of property - it being a period when the lawless elements in Basingstoke were addicted to rioting and were held by the authorities, if held at all, with a very slack rein'. The Basingstoke of Thomas Burberry, with its intolerant population of drunks, rioters and lawbreakers, was far from being a peaceful, settled or united place.

In the *Official Guide to Basingstoke,* published in the early 1920s, it was proudly claimed that, 'as pioneers in a national industry, now employing hundreds of thousands of workpeople and with many million pounds of capital, Burberry's invest the place of origin of their early struggles against prejudice and numerous manufacturing difficulties with local interest, however prosaic, which may well survive more romantic traditions'. It was no doubt 'Old Tom' himself who had provided such heartfelt copy, for his attempts to improve the moral character of the town would not have been universally appreciated or understood. He had probably experienced hostility from fellow shopkeepers. The average Basingstoke tradesman, preferring to drink, smoke and gossip than to advance his business career, may well have envied and resented him for his success.

The extent to which Burberry was at odds with elements in the town was shockingly revealed in the great conflagration that destroyed his Winchester Street shop. At 6 o'clock on the evening of 17 April 1905, one of the assistants, Miss Grey, was lighting the gas lamps in the front window displaying goods from the millinery department. A piece of lightweight material blew on to her taper and caught fire. Soon the whole window was ablaze. With urgent orders to complete, the head dressmaker, Miss Claridge, and twenty-seven female assistants were hard at work at the back of the shop. A male colleague, Mr Beke, attempted to beat out the flames, whilst other staff were hurriedly evacuated, the girls having no time to collect clothing and other possessions from the dormitory above. Beke emerged with singed hair, choking from the smoke. When the Fire Brigade eventually appeared, with its inadequate steam pump, the whole shop frontage, nearly a hundred feet in length, was an inferno.

It was clear to the fire chief, Captain Evans, that the building was already lost. He concentrated on saving the adjoining premises, those of Wagstaff the ironmonger on the west side and of Mr and Mrs Aldous on the east. The dregs of Basingstoke soon gathered outside. According to the correspondent for the *Hants and Berks Gazette,* some of the jeering bystanders casually entered the threatened premises and began to help themselves to Wagstaff's and Aldous's possessions. 'The procedure afforded a good deal of amusement to the crowd in Winchester Street, especially when trunks and portmanteaus handed down from one of the bedroom windows discharged their miscellaneous contents on the heads of the people below.'

Captain Evans eventually ejected the looters, though 'not without receiving some violence'. Salvaged items disappeared into the crowd as barrels of oil and casks of gunpowder were removed from the ironmonger's, 'an occasional explosion in the fire showing that a few cartridges had been left behind'. The reporter noted that melted gold coins were later to be picked up in the ruins. 'Several young ladies found themselves penniless, and had to borrow trifling sums to enable them to wire their friends. Also the limited extent of their wardrobes after the fire was manifest in their personal appearance, but this state of affairs rather added to than detracted from their wonted charms.'

It was as well that Burberry had shifted production to the other end of the street, for Basingstoke depended on the firm for employment. Most of the town's young, unmarried girls aspired to work in the factory. Locals joked that the letters 'BYP' ('Burberry's Yarn Proof'), suspended in large, white tiles over its Hackwood Road entrance, stood for 'Burberry's Young People', since it employed so many of the town's youth. 'Old Tom' kept a sharp eye over them as they sat at the clattering machines, each dressmaker working on a single garment from start to finish, for which she would be paid seven shillings. Though 'a kind and considerate Master, not pampering anyone but rendering to each a just reward for faithful services', Burberry was also strict and puritanical, and intolerant of skylarking. Mrs Margot Woodcock, who was born in 1903 and worked for Burberry in his office, recalled him in 1992 as 'a dear old man ... but one day he had me up to see him and told me I'd have to go as I was too fond of the boys. Oh yes! One day I think I threw something over one of them.' Even such moderately flirtatious behaviour was quite enough to earn her dismissal.

Still preaching almost to the end, Thomas Burberry died at Crossways on 7 April 1926, aged 90. On the day of his burial at South View Cemetery, the municipal flag flew at half-mast over the Town Hall. Basingstoke's debt to Burberry was considerable. His purchase in 1919 of Goldings Park, the private estate that the town intended for a public space in memory of the Great War, was described by his obituarist as 'one of the most beneficent acts of our generation' - for Burberry had undertaken to hold it for the War Memorial Committee while it raised the necessary funds. He may have been driven to such a gesture by his conscience, having profited considerably from wartime concessions. His sorrowing staff remembered him on their wreath as simply 'the kindest of chiefs'.

The firm continued to expand under Burberry's younger son, Arthur Michael. During the Second World War (when the factory was evacuated from Basingstoke), it provided weatherproofs for the services and 'Utility' gabardine rainwear for civilians. Advertising campaigns from the 1920s had emphasised Burberry's associations with the affluent classes and with elegant, leisurely pursuits. The most distinctive of all Burberry products, the Trench Coat, was originally intended for the use of officers in the Great War, but became in the mid-twentieth century a symbol of urban sophistication and *chic*. Indelibly associated with some of the most iconic film-stars of all time, it attains the height of glamour in *Casablanca* (released in 1942), when it is worn by Humphrey Bogart during his most powerful and romantic scenes, and in *Breakfast at Tiffany's* (released in 1961), in the scene in which Audrey Hepburn and George Peppard cavort in the pouring rain in search of 'Cat', each of them sensibly clad in a Burberry Trench Coat. It makes further memorable appearances in the *Pink Panther* series, when it is worn by Peter Sellars in the role of Inspector Cluseau, as it is also by Meryl Streep in *Kramer vs Kramer,* by Michael Douglas in *Wall Street* and by Warren Beatty in *Dick Tracey*.

Arthur Michael Burberry retired in 1951 and the firm was gradually taken over by Great Universal Stores, until by 1966 it had become a wholly-owned subsidiary. Burberry's today is one of the world's leading luxury fashion houses, with stores and franchises in over fifty locations - which include not only Paris, Brussels, Dusseldorf and New York, but also Kuwait, Fiji, Bangalore and Guam.

The Basingstoke factory closed in 1957 and, instead of its coats, the trademark Burberry products are now its fashionable accessories, ranging from handbags and fragrances to watches, jewellery, scarves, umbrellas and luggage. As often as not these have been marked, at least until recently, by the famous 'Burberry Check', the handsome beige, black, white and red tartan which was introduced in 1924 for the lining of the Trench Coat, but which, since 1967, has been widely used to identify the full range of the firm's clothing and accessories.

Thomas Burberry, who presumably gave the check his personal approval, would have been aghast at its association with 'Chavs', to use a slang term which appeared as if from nowhere in 2004 and has since entered common parlance. The word 'chav' is a convenient label for any member, male or female, of the modern British underclass. Aggressive, illiterate, feckless and criminally-minded, 'chavs' are recognisable by their uniform of branded sports or casual clothing, an ensemble that is often completed by a baseball cap.

The 'buzzword of 2004' was helpfully defined for readers of *The Daily Telegraph*. 'Chavs are most at home in run-down, small-town shopping precincts, smoking and shouting at their mates. A teenage single mum chewing gum or drawing on a cigarette as she pushes her baby, Keanu, to McDonald's to meet the chav she believes to be his father is a chavette.' ( 'Keanu', an unattractive Hawaiian name, was popularised by the actor Keanu Reeves, who starred in the *Matrix* films. McDonald's is a chain of restaurants that sells cheap American hamburgers. It has a branch in the Market Place, Basingstoke, next door to Burberry's 'temperance café'.)

The etymology of the term is uncertain. Some have suggested a derivation from *chavi,* the Romany word for a young person. Others have proposed that it is an acronym, standing for 'Council-Housed and Violent'. In December 2004, it was rumoured that the pupils of Cheltenham Ladies College had invented the word (a contraction of 'Cheltenham Average'), as shorthand for any unprepossessing member of the local population. The town's Mayor took great offence ( 'I'm definitely not scum,' he told *The Daily Telegraph*), and their principal had hurriedly to reassure him that the locals were held in great respect by her girls and were never spoken of in derogatory terms.

When the word first became current in 2004, the archetypal chav was said to be an actress called Danniella Westbrook, who had earlier played the role of Samantha Mitchell in the television soap opera *Eastenders*. A native of Essex, Westbrook is a tragic figure whose addiction to cocaine (which she inhaled daily for some years) has caused the total erosion of her nasal septum. She has had several breast enhancements and her personal secrets have been sold to the press. To illustrate her 'chav' credentials, *The Sun* in 2004 published a photograph of Westbrook and her baby, Jodie, both in head-to-toe Burberry check, with a matching buggy and handbag. Whilst Westbrook proudly admits to being a 'chav' - how else could she justify her collection of sixty baseball caps, her weekly manicure and her personal spray-tan machine? - she claims to have intended these outfits as a joke.

The 'chav effect' on the Burberry brand was, however, catastrophic. Hurriedly distancing itself from the stereotype, the firm withdrew its range of branded baseball caps and relegated the Burberry check to its original position, which was on the inner lining of its clothes. The C.E.O. tried to laugh the matter off and reassure shareholders. 'They're yesterday's news. It was mostly counterfeit, and Britain accounts for less than ten per cent of our sales anyway.' When in 2006 a tuk-tuk vehicle was painted in Burberry check and launched, as the 'Chavrolet', on the streets of Brighton, the company was not amused and threatened a lawsuit. They had every reason to be apprehensive. In 2008 *The Sun* conducted a survey of '200 shoppers in the North West' - they were presumably hand-picked for their good taste and knowledge of the history of dress - who voted 'chavvy Burberry check the worst fashion faux-pas for the last 50 years'.

Other prominent figures who have been identified in the press as 'chavs' include an association footballer, Wayne Rooney, and his wife Coleen, a busty model called Jordan, a vapid 'celebrity' called Jade Goody and a singer-turned-television presenter, Kerry Katona. When my book is mouldering on the Local Studies shelves of libraries and in the cloakrooms of country houses across north Hampshire, these names will all, I am sure, have been forgotten.

Burberry's appeal to the fashion sense of such people has been described as 'a sociological example of prole drift, where an up-market product begins to be consumed *en masse* by a lower socio-economic group'. According to a more convincing theory, 'chavs' derive their fashion sense from the distinctively-dressed British football hooligans of the late 1970s and early 1980s who were known as 'Casuals'. Fans of Liverpool F.C., who regularly travelled to the Continent in support of their team, began to be seen in expensive, designer sportswear. As often as not it had been looted from shops during the inevitable violent disturbances of those days. The troublemakers discovered to their delight that, in their designer clothing, they were all but invisible to the police, who were more wary of the traditional 'skinheads' in their Doctor Marten's boots. The 'Casuals' were those canny hooligans who abandoned club colours altogether in favour of designer labels, including Burberry, in order to infiltrate rival groups, enter pubs on match days and generally avoid the attention of the police. Somewhat improbably, their fashion icons are said to have included Sir Edmund Hillary and Ronnie Corbett, both of whom were well known for dressing in Burberry. The 'Casual' look, which, by the 1990s, had become a sort of uniform, no longer fooling the police, has influenced the dress-sense of an entire generation, giving rise in particular to the down-market 'chavvy' style.

It is ironic indeed that the name of the good and blameless Thomas Burberry, who devoted so much time, money and effort to eradicating shameless behaviour in Basingstoke, should thus be associated with an unruly underclass. He would have been as perplexed and troubled by the chavs' lack of self-respect, though, as by the fact that they never seem to possess any sort of raincoat.

*Mr Toad models Burberry*

# II. The Cook and the College

W illiam the Cook of Basingstoke may never have wielded a frying pan in his life. Born in the late 12th century, when surnames were the growing fashion, he was probably the son or grandson of a genuine cook who had prospered in the kitchen. Depending on the employer, cooks enjoyed high status and were often very handsomely rewarded. The Cooks of Basingstoke were of sufficient standing to  intermarry with the local gentry and, as late as 1517, to be buried in the chancel of St Michael's Church.

There were thus the lords of nearby Herriard on the maternal side, including Richard de Herriard, a royal justice under Richard and John, and William's own wife Christina (sometimes known by her mother's surname, FitzAce), a daughter of Walter FitzOliver, whose family were freeholders on the royal manor of Basingstoke. William the Cook farmed the portion of their estate - some sixty scattered acres, mostly in the surrounding open fields - that had been settled on Christina. They lived in the farm-house on the junction of Brook Street and Church Street, opposite the Parsonage, and produced eight children - a son, Walter, born in about 1200, and seven daughters, all of whom survived to adulthood.

Though an only son, Walter was marked out for a clerical education, which he appears to have received at Merton Priory in Surrey, and then at Oxford. Founded in about 1117, Merton was an Augustinian priory, as rich and grand as any in England. Thomas Becket had been to school there, and so, it is thought, had Nicholas Breakspear, better known as Adrian IV, the only Englishman ever to be elected Pope.[2]

2 Merton has since been absorbed into Greater London and, thanks to Henry VIII, the once-mighty Priory has been obliterated from view. Almost all traces of it are buried under a Sainsbury's Savacentre and the equally unlovely Merton Relief Road.

Young Walter's abilities may have been recognised by a local priest who was prepared to sponsor his education. A likely candidate is Philip de Lucy, who was Rector of both Selborne (from 1197) and Basing (from 1204), owing both appointments to the Augustinian canons of Selborne. To these he added a third living (which he held until his death in 1233), the Vicarage of Cuddington in Surrey, to which he was presented by the Prior of Merton.

There were other local men associated with Merton, including Geoffrey and Henry de Basing (himself a future Prior), to whom Walter may have been related. He was certainly connected to the Basings who were rich merchants in the City of London, for whom Basinghall Street is named. Solomon 'de Basings' was Mayor of London in 1216, as was his grandson Adam, the owner of Aldermanbury, in 1251.

Another influence in Walter's life is likely to have been John of Basingstoke, who after Oxford had both studied and taught at Paris, before completing his education in Athens. In 1204, a Crusader army had captured Constantinople and deposed the Byzantine Emperor, whose crown had fallen, 'by the grace of God', to Baldwin of Flanders. Within a year, the Crusaders were the masters also of central and southern Greece. The province of Attica had been allotted to a Burgundian knight, Otto de la Roche, who styled himself Duke of Athens. Visiting the city under his rule, John had befriended members of the local Byzantine aristocracy, of whose learning he was in awe. He was disconcerted to find that the Greek archbishop's teenage daughter, Constantina, was considerably more learned than he, despite his years in Paris. Admittedly she was a prodigy, even a seer. As John often explained to the chronicler Matthew Paris, Constantina had been his 'mistress' and there was nothing he now knew of any value that had not been 'begged' from her.

Refreshingly open-minded, self-deprecating and humorous, John had charm enough to win over the influential Athenians, in spite of the catastrophe that had recently befallen them. He returned with a proficiency in the Greek language that was almost unprecedented in the West, and a store of recondite learning, such as the means of representing numbers by a system of strokes. His later works (all now lost) included translations of Greek religious writings and a useful compendium of Greek grammar. The influential codex containing the *Testaments of the Twelve Patriarchs,* now in Cambridge University Library, probably came to England through his agency, after he had admired it in the Archbishop's library at Athens. This was thought to be a part of the Bible that had been maliciously concealed by the Jews, on the grounds that its prophecies about Christ were uncomfortably accurate.

John of Basingstoke was intimately associated with Bishop Robert Grosseteste of Lincoln, the outstanding scholar and pastor of his day, who appointed him Archdeacon of Leicester in 1235. Grosseteste received instruction in Greek from John, and taught it in turn to the noble boys whom he took into his household, including the two elder sons of Simon de Montfort, Earl of Leicester. The inner circle of Grosseteste's friends included the Dominican Friar and empirical scientist Roger Bacon (another Greek scholar), and the Franciscan Adam Marsh, an internationally-renowned Oxford theologian. To these should be added Simon de Montfort himself, who shared their spiritual outlook and was strictly guided in matters of conscience by Grosseteste and Marsh. Simon certainly knew and admired John of Basingstoke and is said to have been grief-stricken at his death in 1252. He may have had opportunities to see him when at Odiham, his seat in the neighbourhood of Basingstoke, the town being much more to him than a supplier of beer.

Very little is known of Walter's background and early life, but he and John may well have been related. Aged 12 or 13, he is thought, like John, to have proceeded to Oxford, to sit at the feet of the professors who frequented the place, including Adam Marsh. No colleges existed to support undergraduates at that time. Those able to afford it took lodgings in special 'halls', of which St Edmund Hall (now converted into a college) is the sole survivor. Walter is believed to have lodged in Mauger's Hall (now the Golden Cross), in which Merton Priory had an interest.

At Oxford, Walter probably received some training in the Civil Law, after which he applied for holy orders in the diocese of Lincoln. Marsh himself, whose standards were exacting, commended him to Bishop Grosseteste's assistant as an 'honorabilis vir' - a worthy man - and his future was assured. Walter applied his legal and administrative skills in the service of Merton Priory, which in 1233 appointed him to the Vicarage at Cuddington, where he succeeded his supposed mentor, Philip de Lucy of Basing. He was variously described in documents as 'Walter of Basingstoke', 'Walter of Basing, clerk' and 'Walter the clerk', but preferred to be known as 'Walter de Merton'. Having often had contact with the King, however - Henry III was a regular visitor to the Priory, and had also been to Basingstoke in 1226 and 1230 - Walter, the skilled clerk, was rapidly recruited to the royal service.

No clerk would so much as pick up his pen without a fee. At a time when writs were the main instrument of government, a royal clerk could expect to make a very comfortable living indeed, much like a modern Member of the European Parliament, who is guaranteed a minimum of £1.5 million in salary, pension and expenses during each five-year term in office. Walter had ample money to spend by 1240, when he bought the manors of Malden and Chessington with Farleigh in Surrey, together with that of Basingstoke, which the King granted him for five years. He had already added to the family property in the town - an early acquisition had been 'the house called St John's', apparently abutting the farm-house in which he had grown up - and arranged suitable dowries for his sisters. Their husbands were mostly local men, as is evident from their names - Thomas de Worting, Peter de la Clythe (Cliddesden), Richard Elvet (Elvetham), Stak at Wych (Wickham).

As well as his numerous kindred, the entire locality would have known and respected Walter de Merton, who was hardly inconspicuous. About six feet three inches tall (his skeleton has been measured), well built and athletic enough to cover great distances on horseback, he was, to judge from carvings, full-faced, with a strong, shrewd and kindly demeanour, while contemporaries speak of his wisdom, generosity, good-nature and 'bright integrity', which combined to inspire deep loyalty and devotion in others.

Walter was as devoted in turn to his friends, his family and his home town. Determined to be remembered there, he converted 'the house called St John's' (might it have been an old townhouse of the St Johns, lords of Basing?) into a hospital 'for the support of the ministers of the altar of God whose strength is failing, and the wayfaring poor of Christ'. He stated in his charter of foundation that he was acting 'in memory of the laudable life of Lady Christina my mother'. The brethren of the Hospital were to keep the flame of his parents alive in St Michael's Church, by tending the pair of candles that they had set up there.

When Walter's father died in 1238, he inherited the family farm. Having already made ample provision for his sisters, he promptly endowed the Hospital with 'the entire property of my ancestors in Basingstoke', and encouraged further donations. Letters of protection were issued in 1251-2 by the King, and other privileges followed, including a grant from the Papal Legate in 1268, exempting the Hospital from episcopal control. The first two wardens of the Hospital were Henry Cardiff, the parson of Eastrop, and Peter de Abingdon, Walter's lifelong friend. There was to be provision also for a chaplain and a clerk, not to mention other servants.

The tiny chapel of the Hospital (which survived in a dilapidated state until 1778) was a tall flint building with a tiled roof. The interior measurements were only about twelve feet by five. It had stone-mullioned windows and a panelled roof, the intersections of the panels being decorated with tufts of foliage and with shields of the Merton arms. The adjacent house was described in 1697 as 'low, ordinary and mean', whilst the separate infirmary was considered 'extremely dark, and fit for none but those that are distracted'. With an assured income from upwards of 250 acres of land, it is somewhat surprising that more spacious accommodation could not have been provided, there being room for only two poor persons at any one time.

Walter's career had meanwhile taken another turn. By the end of 1242 he had been appointed chancellor to Nicholas Farnham, Bishop of Durham, another Merton protégé who had studied at Oxford and had later become Professor of Medicine at

Paris. Having gained valuable experience and added a clutch of northern benefices to his collection, Walter returned in 1247 to the royal chancery. He became one of the closest advisers to the King and the recipient of occasional gifts from him, such as oaks from the royal forest of Pamber, with which to carry out repairs to his beloved Hospital. From 1258 he regularly deputised for the Chancellor and was Henry's preferred candidate for that office. To appease the barons, however, his appointment had to be deferred until July 1261, when Henry, having politely dismissed the baronial Chancellor, gladly handed over the great seal to Walter.

Walter's tenure of the highest office in the land was, however, brief. When Simon de Montfort seized power in the summer of 1263, he was inevitably removed. His Surrey estates were taken over and pillaged by the rebels, and Walter retired to Bath, of which he was Archdeacon. A year later, having no personal quarrel with Simon and many friends in common, he obtained letters of protection from the baronial party. His estates were restored and, after Simon's defeat at Evesham in 1264, he was adequately compensated for his losses. King Henry employed him in a variety of official roles, though it was not until 1272 that he was reinstated as Chancellor, by the Council governing for the new King, Edward I, then absent on Crusade. The now elderly Walter resigned the office as soon as Edward returned in 1274, having already been elected Bishop of Rochester.

Throughout this period Walter had been preoccupied with another matter, the founding of the Oxford college that was to be his lasting legacy to the world. The French fashion for founding colleges had been promoted in England by William of Sedgefield, a former Professor of Theology at Paris, whom Walter would have known while at Durham. William of Sedgefield's bequest to the University of Oxford was the core endowment of University College, which is thus considered to be Oxford's premier college.

Following William's example, the Bishop of Durham had, in 1260, imposed an unusual penance on John Balliol, King of Scots, in furtherance of which his widow,

Devorguilla, had founded Balliol College. The novelty of Walter's foundation was that it was to be entirely self-supporting and self-governing under a Warden, whose management would be subject to annual scrutiny by the scholars themselves. Originally twenty in number, the scholars were to be selected from Walter's own kin. Spare places were available to candidates from the diocese of Winchester, or from other dioceses in which the college held land. There was scope for increasing the numbers, if and when the college finances allowed. This was highly likely as the college endowments, in addition to the manors in Surrey, were considerable.

The college was at first administered from Malden, where the Warden - Walter appointed his old friend Peter of Abingdon, late of the Basingstoke Hospital - also looked after orphans and younger boys *(parvuli)* from Walter's family. The senior scholars, including no less than eight of Walter's nephews, were accommodated at Bull Hall, off St Aldate's, while pursuing their studies in the schools. By the end of 1268, however, Walter had bought up an acre plot in the south-east corner of the city, between St John's Lane (now Merton Street) and the walls, on which to raise permanent college buildings and a chapel. Walter lived to see the erection of the Hall of Merton College, which dates from the early 1270s, and the creation of Oxford's earliest quadrangle, known as 'Mob Quad'. Definitive statutes were issued in 1274, whereby the entire collegiate body was established in Oxford. The existing Muniment Room and Chapel were completed in the 1290s.

Now Bishop of Rochester, though seldom there, Walter continued to lead an active and busy life. He was at Oxford in the spring of 1277, accompanying the Archbishop of Canterbury, the college patron, on an official visit, and thence travelled to Durham for the last time. On his return journey he fell from his horse while fording a river, probably at Sulby in Northamptonshire. He died soon afterwards, on 27 October 1277.

Walter de Merton was a true pioneer in that he had founded the first wholly self-governing university college in England, the model for all subsequent colleges. He also introduced the system whereby the preferred candidates for scholarships and fellowships were to be the founder's own kin. His example was closely followed by Robert Eglesfield, the founder of Queen's College in 1340, and by William of Wykeham, the founder, in 1379, of New. These men saw it as their duty to provide for their kindred in one way or another. After all, each college had been richly endowed with property that would otherwise have been left to them. There was no shame in nepotism.

Walter had further provided for his family in his immensely complicated will and by gift in his lifetime. As a special favour, Henry III had allowed him by 1256 to create a separate manor out of the royal lands at Basingstoke, of which he had recently been the tenant. In 1262-3, Walter settled this property on a nephew, Walter Oliver. The manor of Basingstoke Merton, or 'Watermartens' (*i.e.* 'Walter Merton's'), comprised by 1311 of nearly 300 acres, had subsequently descended to Maud, daughter and heiress of Walter's nephew Thomas de Worting. Maud married William Tauke, and the male line of their family held the manor for many generations, until the death of John Tauke in 1503. John Tauke's great-great-nephew, William Fisher, sold Watermartens in 1593 to Richard Deane, and in 1714, having passed through various families, it was bought by William Russell, a lawyer, who served between 1745 and 1761 as Recorder of Basingstoke.

Russell demolished the old manor-house, 'Taukes', and named its grand replacement 'Bedford House', in honour of his putative kinsman, the Duke of Bedford. It was conspicuous in the row of fine buildings in Church Street that was obliterated in 1967. The site is marked today by the Great Wall of Basingstoke. The manorial farm-house of Watermartens, however, appears to be the Tudor building behind the church that has miraculously survived. This is now known as Church Cottage.

Ironically, Walter's kinsfolk took so half-hearted an interest in their privileged status at Oxford that eventually they forgot that they were even related to him and, by sheer neglect, allowed their privileges to lapse, although they were only formally abolished by

Statute in 1854. To take up one of the scholarships meant committing oneself to a life of celibacy and contemplation. Many of Walter's kin, like the Taukes, were perhaps not cut out to be clerks, preferring careers in farming or business. Those branches of the family that provided scholars were doomed to extinction, for they were expected never to marry. The last three elections of kinsmen were in 1462, 1482 and 1487. Subsequent candidates received scant encouragement from the college. The rejection of an application by Richard Fisher in 1577 was reversed on appeal, but on grounds other than his pedigree.

The sons of Walter's sister Matilda were surnamed Portsmouth, a name that has persisted in Basingstoke and the locality. Curiously, a family of Portsmouths were the 19th-century tenants of Merton Farm, living on the exact site where Walter had grown up and founded his hospital. Edmund Portsmouth, whose father and grandfather had farmed at Sherborne St John, held 390 acres in 1851. Edmund's son Henry had increased the holding by 1861 to 1,050 acres, and served as Mayor in 1875-6. When the college sold Henry the freehold in 1887, it may unwittingly have restored it to the ownership of Walter's family. The philistine Henry lost no time in sweeping away the untidy remnants of the Hospital.

It seems also that descendants of Merton's maternal aunt Margaret FitzOliver, many of whom would have been eligible for Founder's Kin scholarships, can be traced to the present day. Margaret married William Chastayne de Kingsmill by whom she had at least nine children. From 1234 onwards, variously called William 'Chasteyne', 'son of Castana' and even 'Shaftein', he appears in a number of charters relating to Selborne Priory. He is said in them to own a house in Basing and land at 'Todefforde' (Toad Ford) in Basingstoke. It is clear that his father or some other recent ancestor was called Castana. One of his daughters was called Castania, which sounds like the Latin word for a chestnut-tree.

The 'Chastaynes' or Castons were represented in Basingstoke, pursuing various trades, at least until the 19th century. By 1808 George Caston kept an ironmonger's shop on the site of the Town Hall, which is clearly depicted in a contemporary painting. By 1820 he had moved the business to larger premises on the south side of the Market Place, directly opposite his old shop, where McDonald's is currently located. In a foundry at the rear, Caston branched into the production of agricultural machinery. The business was later bought by the Wallis family and removed to Station Hill, where it continued (as Wallis and Steevens) until 1967, but the original owners are remembered in Caston's Yard.

The 'Kingsmill' branch of the family was more eminent. According to tradition, their Chastayne ancestor, perhaps William himself, had saved the life of King John while hunting. His reward was a grant of the King's Mill in Basingstoke. Hugh de Kingsmill, William's eldest son by Margaret, Walter de Merton's aunt, was cited before the Bailiffs of Basingstoke in 1277, having rashly attempted to sell it without a licence. The mill was taken back into the hands of the Crown, but the name Kingsmill had stuck, and three millrinds remain in the family's arms.

By 1327 the Kingsmills, putative descendants of Hugh or one of his brothers, had acquired a country estate centred on Arborfield Cross in Berkshire - with their seat, probably of the open-hall type, on the site of Langley Pond Farm at Barkham - but without having relinquished their property or interests in Basingstoke. Richard Kingsmill of Barkham was Bailiff of the town in 1456, as was his elder son, also Richard. In 1491, the younger Richard's property in Basingstoke included two houses in Church Street called 'Cayys' and 'Oxys' and a mill called 'Fynceys', though he resided on the south side of Winchester Street, most of which he also owned.

Richard's house was grand enough to accommodate Katherine of Aragon and her entourage in early November 1501. A charming, naïve sixteen-year-old, Katherine was bound for London where she was to marry Arthur, Prince of Wales. Her exhausting and bewildering journey to the altar had begun at Granada on 21 May, when her parents, King Ferdinand and Queen Isabella, had sent her on her way, not expecting ever to see her again. After travelling for weeks across Spain's rugged heartland, Katherine had ventured, on 17 August, into a stormy Bay of Biscay. Tossed around for a terrifying three weeks, her fleet had been driven back to the Spanish shore. Eventually, on 2 October, it had scraped into Plymouth with an English escort.

Katherine's itinerary had been meticulously planned, and Richard Kingsmill had known when to expect her. The people of Basingstoke have long relied on royal visits for excitement and, on this occasion, they would not have been disappointed. If they were anything like the Londoners, they would have given Katherine 'a tremendous ovation'. However, Thomas More was to be struck by the 'ludicrous' appearance of her escort. 'Except for three, or at the most four, of them, they were just too much to look at: hunchback, undersized, barefoot pygmies from Ethiopia … you would have thought they were refugees from hell.'

After a single night in Basingstoke, Katherine continued her journey to Dogmersfield, where she was the guest of the Bishop of Bath and Wells. Katherine was under strict instructions to have no dealings with Arthur until the day of her wedding, but an impatient Henry VII insisted on meeting her there with the prince. He seemed satisfied with the bride. The wedding took place at St Paul's Cathedral on 14 November and - famously unconsummated, despite the 15-year-old Arthur's boasting - was an event that changed the course of history.

In his will of 1511, Richard Kingsmill desired to be buried in the chancel of St Michael's Church, next to Alice his wife. Their grandchildren included William Kingsmill 'de Basing', the last Prior of St Swithun's in Winchester, and Morwetha, the last Abbess of Wherwell. Another grandson, Sir John Kingsmill, being one of the commissioners for the dissolution of such monasteries, acquired much of the spoil locally, including, in 1540, the manor of Sydmonton, a former possession of the Abbey of Romsey. Sir John resided at Sydmonton and was buried in 1556 in nearby Kingsclere Church. He is commemorated, with his seventeen children, in a brass in the Kingsmill Chapel, which was regrettably converted in 1978 into a kitchen and meeting room. Coincidentally, the rectory of Kingsclere had (from 1261) been one of the many livings held by his ancestor Walter de Merton.[3]

3 Until 1322, a branch of the Caston family owned the adjacent hall house, forerunner of the present Falcon House, which, now bent with age, is one of Kingsclere's most historic buildings.

A grandson of Sir John, William Kingsmill, handsomely rebuilt Sydmonton Court in red brick. Like others of his line he enjoyed close links with the royal family. When Queen Elizabeth came to Basing in 1601, a glittering French embassy, 400-strong, had to be separately quartered at the Vyne. William is probably to be counted among 'the willing and obedient people of Hampshire' who, 'upon two days' warning', brought suitable beds and furniture for their use. Reporting afterwards to the grateful Queen at Basing, they queued up to be knighted.

Perhaps the most distinguished member of the family was Sir William's granddaughter, Anne Kingsmill, the sometime maid of honour to Mary of Modena, Duchess of York, and wife from 1684 of Colonel Heneage Finch, later Earl of Winchilsea. Born at Sydmonton in 1661 - the family had, by that time, disposed of all its Basingstoke property, sold in its entirety to the Paulets - Anne was remarkably well-educated and a skilled poet. Poetry writing was not, however, considered to be suitable for a woman and those who discovered Anne's secret, apart from her sympathetic husband, tended to make fun of her. Pope, evidently unnerved by her skill, derides her in a play, *Three Hours after Marriage,* in which she appears as Phoebe Clinket. Eventually she dared to publish a miscellany of her verse, one of the first such publications by a woman. Thanks to Wordsworth, who re-discovered it and praises it in *Lyrical Ballads,* her reputation was assured.

The direct male line of the Kingsmills died out in 1766 in the person of William, a certified lunatic. His niece Elizabeth, a dwarf, married a naval officer, 25 years her junior, who adopted the name. Their descendants remained at Sydmonton until 1975. Sydmonton Court, overlooking Watership Down and surrounded by a vast estate, is where Andrew, the Lord Lloyd-Webber of Sydmonton, is now sumptuously housed. There are many thousands of traceable descendants of the Kingsmills through the female line, the likely progeny of Walter de Merton's aunt. They include Patrick Macnee, the actor who played John Steed in *The Avengers,* the sports journalist Clare Balding, who grew up at Kingsclere, the 'dot com' millionairess Martha Lane Fox - and the present writer.

Like the family itself, Basingstoke has made little of its connection with Walter de Merton, though a monstrous development to the north of the town is to be called 'Merton Rise', presumably in his honour. The college founded by Basingstoke's most famous son, which has produced four Nobel prize winners, the mathematician who solved Format's last theorem, the physician who discovered the circulation of blood and the founder of the Bodleian Library, is equally neglectful of Basingstoke.

*Something to be proud of? The birthplace of Walter de Merton*

# III. Druggets and Shalloons

*The yard of the Crown Inn, now Joice's Yard*

In the late morning of Friday 26 October 1798, a mud-spattered stage-coach drew into the yard of the Crown Inn in Winchester Street, Basingstoke. An elderly clergyman alighted from it, along with his daughter, a maid of 23. A tall, slim, upright girl with hazel eyes and dark, curly hair, she was somewhat careless of her appearance and was generally considered to be attractive rather than beautiful. Her nose and mouth were small, and her doll-like cheeks were apt to glow healthily with emotion or exertion. She had a bright, animated expression and a quick, decisive step, suggestive of great spirit. Her face veritably sparkled on occasion with intelligence and humour. Unusually for a young gentlewoman, her chief interest was in literary composition. She had already written two novels, not with a view to publication but for her own pleasure and for the entertainment of her family during the long evenings by the fireside. The novels were called *Elinor and Marianne* and *First Impressions*. Years later they were to be published under different titles - *Sense and Sensibility* and *Pride and Prejudice* - and, with other books that followed, were to make the name of the young authoress, Jane Austen, famous throughout the world.

Emerging into the yard of the Crown she seemed tired and subdued, for reasons that were soon apparent. As the stiff figure of her mother was hauled from the coach, it was plain that she had been overlong in the company of a hypochondriac, who had never ceased to complain about the discomforts of the journey and its effects on her health. The family had passed a pleasant summer with relatives in East Kent. Their return journey to the Rectory at Steventon, seven miles west of Basingstoke, took four days. There had been three overnight stops at inns along the way - at Sittingbourne, Dartford and Staines. At the Bull and George in Dartford on Wednesday, Jane had had to share a double bed with her mother, who had forced down a hearty meal and, as Jane reported to her sister Cassandra, 'now seems quite stout'. At Staines, however, 'my Mother began to suffer from the exercise & fatigue of travelling so far, & she was a good deal indisposed from that particular kind of evacuation which has generally preceded her Illnesses'. By the time they arrived at Basingstoke, it was only her sense of humour, and the prospect of writing an ironic account of the journey to her beloved sister, that had kept Jane from reaching the end of her tether.

There was an interval of 'more than half an hour' before the coach set off again, on the Andover road, to deposit them at Deane, the closest stop to Steventon. Mrs Austen 'received much comfort from a Mess of Broth', and had time for a quick consultation with her doctor, John Lyford, who was summoned from his house at 1 New Street. A tall, fine-looking gentleman of her own generation (they were both about sixty), who persisted in wearing an old-fashioned wig, Lyford gravely recommended that she take twelve drops of laudanum before bed, 'as a Composer'. Jane relished the prospect of administering the dose, which promised to knock her mother out for an entire day. As she wryly observed, 'It is by no means wonderful that her Journey should have produced some Kind of visitation; I hope a few days will entirely remove it.' Lyford was also consulted about the efficacy of some Dandelion Tea that Mrs Austen had recently purchased, 'the receipts for which were shewn him at Basingstoke, & he approved of them highly; they will only require some slight alteration to be better adapted to my Mother's Constitution'.

Meanwhile, Jane had stolen away to do some shopping. 'While my Mother and Mr Lyford were together, I went to Mrs Ryders, & bought what I intended to buy, but not in much perfection. There were no narrow Braces for Children, & scarcely any netting silk; but Miss Wood as usual is going to Town very soon, & will lay in a fresh stock.' Perhaps the shop-women had gossiped about the excitement of a few days before, when the invalid King George had passed through the town, on his way from Weymouth to Windsor, and crowds of local people had gathered to cheer him. It would not have compensated for an unsatisfactory shopping trip. 'I gave 2s/3d a yard for my flannel, & I fancy it is not very good; but it is so disgraceful & contemptible an article in itself, that it's being comparatively good or bad is of little importance. I bought some Japan Ink likewise, & next week shall begin my operations on my hat, on which You know my principal hopes of happiness depend.'

After heavy rain, the road from Staines had been 'disgracefully dirty'. Steventon lane, a shockingly bad road at the best of times, had had 'its full share of it', and, having arrived there later that afternoon, Jane once again found herself a virtual prisoner in her home. The family had recently 'laid down' their own carriage, which had proved to be a luxury beyond their means. Her difficulty was negotiating the sodden, rutted track from the Rectory in order to reach the Deane Gate Inn, which was the nearest coach stop. 'I do not know when I shall be able to get to Deane', she told Cassandra. The main road which passed through Deane was, by contrast, efficiently maintained by the Andover and Basingstoke Turnpike Trust, the travellers paying for repairs with their tolls. The coaches that sped along it eventually rumbled into Basingstoke High Street by way of Sarum Hill.

Other wheeled traffic converged on the High Street from every direction, for Basingstoke was strategically placed at the crossing of five major roads, despite being a tiny place, its population of 2,589 (in 1801) occupying a mere 501 houses (a further 11 were uninhabited).[4]    There were regular Royal Mail and commercial stage-coach services to and from Southampton, Salisbury, Exeter, Taunton, Bath and Bristol, as well as 'light coaches' and lumbering waggons that, for a price, delivered passengers and goods to the nearby towns and villages. London could be reached in six hours, by the road that the Austens had taken from Staines, known today as the A30 but historically as 'the great western road'. Basingstoke was thus the funnel for most of the traffic to and from the West of England. It always had been, but there had never been traffic of such density. The introduction of the stage-coach had marked a revolution in public transport. It was swift, efficient and affordable to all classes, even if poorer travellers had to cling perilously to the roof, with their feet dangling over the edge, or perch in the luggage basket that hung from the back, at the risk of being knocked about, of falling off or even, in winter, of freezing to death, a not infrequent occurrence.

So much heavy traffic thundering through Basingstoke, much of it in the small hours, had altered the character, if not the appearance of the town. In the early 1600s, before the introduction of the stage-coach, the tranquil High Street had been lined with the town-houses of the local gentry, men like Sir James Deane, lord of the manor of Basingstoke, who had 'amassed a large fortune as a merchant adventurer to India, China and the Spice Islands'. Deane had refused to serve as an Alderman in London, but was devoted to Basingstoke, where he founded an almshouse 'for eight poor aged men and women'. Deane's town-house, on the south-west corner of the Market Place, was an impressive timber-framed building with a jettied, brick front, panelled rooms and a tall archway in the middle that led to a courtyard and capacious stables at the rear. Adjoining it on the west side was a similar mansion, believed to be that of the Kingsmill family, where they had entertained Katherine of Aragon for the night in November 1501. It, too, had a jettied, brick front, and a central archway giving access to the rear.

[4] A startling figure: until 2010, it was government policy to increase the size of the town by *945* houses a year!

In the age of the stage-coach, such buildings ceased to be desirable as private residences, but lent themselves perfectly for conversion into coaching-inns. Deane's house was transformed into the 'Angel', whilst Kingsmill's, sold out the family and added to the great estates of the Paulets, marquesses of Winchester and dukes of Bolton, became (by 1671) the 'Maidenhead'. There was sufficient business for four rival concerns. They were the Crown on Winchester Street, almost opposite the Maidenhead, whose surviving archway leads into what is now Joice's Yard; the Feathers at the top of Wote Street; the Wheatsheaf in Winton Square; and the Red Lion in London Street, which all survive. By Jane Austen's time, thirty-seven coaches a day drew up at these six inns to change horses. Stabling had therefore to be provided for a minimum of 148 horses, and it was the Angel, which claimed to have stabling for nearly a hundred, that handled the largest number.

The Angel was kept by William Curtis and his son Richard, who described themselves as 'coachmakers and farmers'. They were a dynamic partnership, whose business included the nearby George Hotel in London Street, the Blackboy Tavern in Church Street, a number of inns in surrounding parishes and over 500 acres of farmland, mainly leased from Lord Bolton but including the 194-acre Basingstoke estate of Merton College, Oxford, centred on the fork between the Kingsclere and Aldermaston roads. Jane Austen's nephew, Edward Austen-Leigh, says of the Curtises that they 'farmed largely' and were keen foxhunters, regularly riding with Mr Chute's pack from the Vyne. William, he tells us, was 'by far the most constant attendant in the field, and … often useful in assisting the hounds'.[5]

The Curtises and their rivals at the other main inns were contractors for the various coach companies. They took pride in the efficiency of their pairs of horse-handlers and ostlers, their coachmen, harness-makers, wheelwrights and farriers, who stood in readiness at all hours of the day and night and could harness an appropriately-matched

5 'The town of Basingstoke supplied several foxhunters', including James Warne, the attorney, 'more than one of the May family, and now and then, between one patient and another, Mr Charles Lyford the surgeon' (son of the old doctor, who was no huntsman), along with 'a large number of Tubbs and other farmers, all keen sportsmen, and some of them good ones'.

team of four horses in as little as three minutes. The approaching coaches announced themselves with trumpet blasts and clattered into the cobbled yards of the inns with much shouting and neighing of horses. In 1824, it is recorded that the Royal Mail departed from the Angel nightly at 12.30, and for Exeter and Plymouth at 2 a.m. 'Light coaches' left for London at 5, 8, 11 a.m. and at 12.30 and 2.15 p.m., and for Exeter at 2 and 10 p.m. There were also regular waggon services to London and other distant towns, and those of the 'carriers', such as H. Jones and Dawes & Co., who inexpensively transported goods and passengers to the surrounding towns and villages.[6] With plenty of additional business from individual horsemen and the owners of private carriages, there was never a moment's peace in Basingstoke.

The coach that the Austens caught at Staines is not identified, nor is the inn at which they alighted, although, writing to Cassandra in East Kent in October 1800, Jane anticipates her stopping at the Crown on her return journey. Characteristic of the coaches serving Basingstoke was the 'Salisbury Flying Machine, hung on steel springs', which set out from the 'Bell Savage' on Ludgate Hill, in the City of London, at ten o'clock each night, arriving at Basingstoke by one o'clock the next day. Horses were changed at the Red Lion, where a late breakfast could also be taken. There was no such thing as lunch in those days; the Austens habitually breakfasted late, bracing themselves for a hefty dinner at 3.30. The Flying Machine would previously have stopped at the Black Dog, Bellfound, and at the White Hart, Blackwater, for changes, but care was taken 'not to stop at unnecessary Places', which included Staines.

With their constant noise and bustle, the coaching inns must have dominated the life of the town. They also played a critical role in Jane Austen's social life. The regular assemblies or balls that she attended from the age of seventeen were organised by Mrs Mary Martin, proprietress of the Maidenhead, and later by William Wilson of the Crown, who in March 1798 assumed the management of both establishments. The

6 In November 1800, Jane Austen's brother Edward had a mangle conveyed from Kent to Basingstoke in a series of such vehicles, for their brother James to arrange delivery to his own house.

assemblies took place in the Town Hall, on the west side of the Market Place (neither inn had sufficient space for them to be held on their own premises),[7] and were a rich source of material for Jane's novels.

Basingstoke's medieval 'Mote' or Town Hall had been destroyed by fire in 1656. Within a year it had been very handsomely rebuilt in brick, rather than wood, though to a similar plan - a large upper floor supported on pillars, with space for a covered market below. Beautifully symmetrical, the building had a steep, tiled roof surmounted by a clock tower. The bell in the tower, donated by the Duke of Bolton in the late 1600s, was used to summon the aldermen and councillors to their meetings. The twice-yearly Basingstoke Petty Sessions alternated between the Town Hall and the Maidenhead, and the magistrates convened there every Tuesday to administer summary justice, though seldom with recourse to the stocks and whipping post outside, which families like the Austens would have considered barbaric.

The elegant Assembly Rooms on the upper floor were also available for public hire, for such gatherings as dinners and balls. The 'Annual Ball' that was held there in January, and the 'Club Ball' in October, were private affairs. The Hants Club was an informal dining club, made up of the local gentlemen, whose regular meetings took place at the Maidenhead and later at the Crown. It may have inspired the 'Club' at Highbury in *Emma*, which also meets at an inn called the 'Crown'. Between 1792 and 1801, Jane Austen had the opportunity to attend between four and eight balls a year, including the exclusive Club Balls, and others that were advertised as 'Subscription Assemblies', but were equally 'open to Nonsubscribers'. They took place mainly in the winter months, though an extra ball was sometimes held in June, in honour of the King's birthday. A ball that is held at the Crown in Highbury, and the assembly at Meryton at which Elizabeth Bennet first encounters Darcy, and is 'obliged, by the scarcity of gentlemen, to sit down for two dances', are clearly modelled on the

[7] The Angel had a substantial outhouse, the upper floor of which had been elegantly fitted as a ballroom, with tall, sash windows, double-doors, handsome chimney pieces and fine, even planking. There is no evidence that Jane Austen ever danced there.

Basingstoke ball.

In the winters of 1793-4 and 1794-5, Jane would surely have danced with the young officers of the South Devon Militia, under Colonel Rolle, who were quartered in the town. The presence of such men (Mrs Chute of the Vyne refers in her diary to their making 'a great fracas') added considerable zest to the rather dreary lives of the provincials. In *Pride and Prejudice,* the officers of the Blankshire Regiment, quartered in Meryton, are mostly friends of Darcy and Bingley, who describe them as 'in general a very creditable, gentlemanlike set'. If they were all as good looking as George Wickham, it is no wonder that they were popular with the local ladies; Kitty Bennet is almost beside herself with excitement. According to the authoress Mary Russell Mitford, Jane Austen herself was, at that time, 'the prettiest, silliest, most affected husband-hunting butterfly she ever remembered', though her description is not entirely convincing.

Jane first refers to her attendance at a ball in a letter dated 25 November 1798, a month or so after her harrowing journey from Kent. 'The ball on Thursday was a very small one indeed,' she tells Cassandra. 'There were but seven couples, and only twenty-seven people in the room.' Since March, the Town Hall balls had been organised by William Wilson of the Crown, but not as well as they had been by Mrs Martin. According to Jane, 'Our assemblies have very kindly declined ever since we laid down the carriage, so that dis-convenience and dis-inclination to go have kept pace together'. Perhaps she had grown tired of seeing the same old faces. On 18 December she anticipated the next ball being 'very stupid, there will be nobody worth dancing with, & nobody worth talking to but Catherine … People get so horridly poor & economical in this part of the World, that I have no patience with them. - Kent is the only place for happiness, Everybody is rich there.'

The effort of getting there might have discouraged Jane from attending altogether, but she was able to stay with her friend Catherine Bigg, the daughter of Lovelace Bigg-Wither, at Manydown Park, which was on the main Andover road and within easy reach of Basingstoke. 'Our ball was very thin,' she reported to Cassandra on Christmas Eve,

*'but by no means unpleasant. - There were 31 people & only 11 ladies out of the Number, & but five single women in the room. - Of the Gentlemen present You may have some idea from a list of my Partners. Mr Wood, G. Lefroy, Rice, a Mr Butcher (belonging to the Temples, a sailor & not of the 11th Light Dragoons), Mr Temple (not the horrid one of all) Mr Wm Orde (Cousin to the Kingsclere Man) Mr John Harwood & Mr Calland, who appeared as usual with his hat in his hand, & stood every now & then behind Catherine & me to be talked to & abused for not dancing. - We teized him however into it at last; - I was very glad to see him again after so long a separation, & he was altogether rather the Genius & Flirt of the Evening. - He enquired after You. - There were twenty Dances & I danced them all, & without any fatigue. - I was glad to find myself capable of dancing so much & with so much satisfaction as I did; - from my slender enjoyment of the Ashford Balls, (as Assemblies for dancing) I had not thought myself equal to it, but in cold weather & with few couples I fancy I could just as well dance for a week together as for half an hour. - My black Cap was openly admired by Mrs Lefroy, & secretly I imagine by every body else in the room.'*

Jane's next ball, on 17 January 1799, was 'chiefly made up of Jervoises and Terrys, the former of whom were apt to be vulgar, the latter to be noisy'. Her 'odd set of partners' included the gangling Dr Lyford, though she felt it was 'a very pleasant evening'. The ball on 30 October 1800 was 'still more good than pleasant, for there were nearly 60 people, & sometimes we had 17 couples'. The mad Earl of Portsmouth (whose seat was at Hurstbourne Park, near Andover), Lord Dorchester (the former commander-in-chief in America, friend of Wolfe, and now tenant of Kempshott Park) and Lord Bolton (of Hackwood Park, son-in-law of the last duke) attended, in spite of which there was a scarcity of 'good men'. Jane had to partner Catherine for four of her nine dances.

Absent from home in November 1800, Jane writes: 'I have charged my Myrmidons to send me an account of the Basingstoke Ball; I have placed my spies at different places that they may collect the more; & by so doing, by sending Miss Bigg to the Townhall itself, & posting my mother at Steventon I hope to derive a good general idea of the whole'. Their subsequent reports suggest that 'the Basingstoke Balls are certainly in decline', which is just as well, as the family were to move to Bath. Jane soon attended her first ball in its grand Assembly Rooms, at which 'there were people enough I suppose to have made five or six very pretty Basingstoke assemblies', but the town is 'vapour, shadow, smoke & confusion'. The move had come as a great shock to her and her tone is of regret for the old days, and for those intimate affairs in the Town Hall at Basingstoke, where everyone had been known to her, and of which she had been pleased to affect so slight an opinion.

Jane's shopping trips to Basingstoke, their regularity constrained by the expense and difficulty of travel, are sparsely documented, but appear to have afforded her little enjoyment. On Friday 7 November 1800, her sister-in-law, Mary Austen, had driven her 'all in the rain to Basingstoke, & still more all in the rain back again'. It had been 'a day of great business with me'. The following February she writes: 'My visit to Miss Lyford begins tomorrow, & ends on Saturday, when I shall have an opportunity of returning here at no expence as the Carriage must take Cath[erine Bigg] to Basingstoke'.

The town was nevertheless the source of most necessities, from the ink with which she wrote to the bed on which she slept: in 1794, Mr Austen had bought two new tent beds for his daughters from John Ring, the Basingstoke auctioneer and furnisher, each with cotton curtains in blue and white check. Ring, who rated himself a 'Gentleman' and was five times Mayor of Basingstoke, had succeeded in 1772 to the upholstery business and property of his father, a joiner and cabinet-maker. His brother William was also in trade in the town, as a grocer. John Ring's house in lower Church Street, beyond the churchyard, still survives (it is currently occupied by Office Angels, a recruitment agency), but his upholstery shop may have been in separate premises which he owned on the opposite (east) side of the same street. It was much frequented by members of the Austen family.

From the two volumes of customer accounts and an accounts ledger, roughly kept by Ring from 1781 to his death in July 1796, which are preserved in the Hampshire Archives, it is evident that he was the main supplier of furnishings to the local gentry, his customers including Jane Austen's father and eldest brother and most of their circle, such as William Chute of the Vyne, John Harwood of Deane and Lovelace Bigg-Wither of Manydown. At the time of his marriage in March 1792, the Rev. James Austen furnished his entire house at Deane from Ring's, with purchases ranging from 'scrub brushes', pails and chamber pots to mirrors and an expensive dining table. Ring could also provide men to hang the wallpaper and lay the carpets that he sold, seamstresses to make the curtains and carpenters to carry out repairs and alterations. It seemed that one could buy, or indeed rent, anything from Ring, whether new or second-hand. He even procured a bidet (or 'biddet') for a demanding customer, despite such devices being associated in English minds with the loose morals of the French.

The Rev. George Austen paid £21-1-0, quite a considerable sum, for his daughters' beds, with their furnishings, which he ordered on 20 January 1794. Cassandra being 21 and Jane having just turned 18, they had outgrown their former beds. On 5 December, Mr Austen returned to Ring's to purchase, for £0-12-0, 'a Small Mahogany Writing Desk with 1 Long Drawer and Glass Ink Stand, Compleat', probably as a present for Jane's nineteenth birthday on 16 December. Unlike the beds, Jane Austen's portable writing desk, presumably the one bought by her father at Ring's, has been preserved. Cassandra, who inherited it in 1817, left it in 1845 to her great-nephew and great-niece William and Mary Austen-Leigh, from whom it eventually passed to Joan Austen-Leigh, co-founder in 1979 of the Jane Austen Society of North America. Miss Austen-Leigh, who for years kept it in an old suitcase in a cupboard at her home in Victoria, British Columbia, presented the desk in 1999 to the British Library, where it is a prized exhibit. It is much as described in Ring's ledger, with its storage space for paper, quills and ink pots. When closed, it is about the size of an old-fashioned typewriter, but it opens up to expose a leather writing surface, which slopes at an ergonomically correct angle. In the two years that followed her nineteenth birthday, Jane Austen put it to good use, writing *Lady Susan, Elinor and Marianne* and *First Impressions.* The desk accompanied her on all her subsequent travels, and, once settled at Chawton, she used it for all her later work, including *Mansfield Park, Emma* and *Persuasion.* That modest piece of Basingstoke craftsmanship had been a constant and reassuring feature of her life. Its contribution to her literary achievement is beyond doubt.

Less satisfactorily, Jane shopped for clothes at Basingstoke, and particularly resented having to depend on Mrs Rider for haberdashery. 'The Neighbourhood have quite recovered the death of Mrs Rider,' she wrote in January 1801, 'so much so, that I think they are rather rejoiced at it now; her Things were so very dear! - & Mrs Rogers [her successor] is to be all that is desirable. Not even Death itself can fix the friendship of the World.' In January 1799 she went to Basingstoke in search of linen for her brother Charles, and 'Mrs Davies frightened him into buying a piece of Irish'. However, she remarks in October 1808 that the town is poor for tailoring; and it seems to be perpetually associated with bad weather. 'Poor Basingstoke Races!' she writes in October 1813, 'there seem to have been two particularly wretched days on purpose for them'.

Occupying creaky timber-framed buildings along the High Street and Market Place, the shopkeepers typically presented enticing displays of their wares in the front windows. As often as not these were bay windows, each with small panes of glass set in a dense framework of mullions. According to Defoe, who had passed this way in 1728, Basingstoke had recently expanded its industry from a thriving corn market to the manufacture of 'Druggets and Shalloons and such slight goods which, however, employs a good number of the poor People, and enables them to get their Bread, which knew not how to get it before'. Druggets and shalloons (named for Châlons in France) are varieties of thin, woollen cloth that were worn only by the poor. It is no wonder that Jane Austen found the town disappointing for tailoring. A visitor in 1795 had also referred to the 'great market for all sorts of corn', as well as to there 'being great trade in malt, as there is in druggets, shalloons etc.' By 1805 the trade in druggets and shalloons had ceased: 'The malting business is however carried on to a considerable extent, and employs a great number of persons.'

The town was sufficiently small for Jane Austen to have had many friends there and to have recognised many faces in the street. Apart from Mrs Rider the haberdasher and Ann Davies the linendraper, there were 'Mrs Skeete', presumably the widow of Richard Skeate, a former Mayor of Basingstoke, whose marriage in 1799 to Mr French, the Reading chemist, is duly reported to Cassandra; and Mrs Francis Russell of Goldings, a far wealthier widow, who appears at the balls. Another Basingstoke acquaintance was the amiable Mrs Martin, formerly of the Maidenhead Inn. As well as taking over the haberdashery and millinery business of John Chambers, she had, in December 1798, invited subscriptions to a new circulating library. Jane informs Cassandra:

*'I have received a very civil note from Mrs Martin requesting my name as a Subscriber to her Library which opens the 14ᵗʰ of January, & my name, or rather Yours is accordingly given. - My mother finds the Money. - Mary subscribes too, which I am glad of, but hardly suspected. - As an inducement Mrs Martin tells us that her Collection is not to consist only of Novels, but of every kind of Literature &c &c. She might have spared this pretension to our family, who are great Novel-readers & not ashamed of being so; but it was necessary I suppose to half her Subscribers.'*

Sadly, Jane has to report in October 1800 that her business has collapsed, and that Mr Wilson, her successor at the Maidenhead, appears also to be in difficulties.

*'Our whole Neighbourhood is at present very busy grieving over poor Mrs Martin, who has totally failed in her business, & had very lately an execution in her house. - Her own brother & Mr Rider are the principal creditors, & they have seized her effects in order to prevent other*

*people's doing it. - There has been the same affair going on, we are told, at Wilson's, & my hearing nothing of you makes me apprehensive that You, your fellow travellers & all your effects, might be seized by the Bailiffs when you stopt at the Crown and sold altogether for the benefit of the creditors.'*

Mrs Martin was widely appreciated for her organisation of the balls, and had many influential friends. Such a 'Friend', indeed, promptly opened a fund for her relief. In an open letter, describing her situation as 'disastrous', he appealed to 'the Benevolent' for donations. The Austen girls, who had helped their old schoolmistress at Reading when she was in similar distress, are sure to have responded.

Mrs Martin, the Curtises and the Rings were exceptional. The Basingstoke tradesmen were not generally noted for their drive or business acumen. The quality of their wares was poor, their prices were high and they seemed incapable of laying in sufficient stock. The range of goods on offer was limited, dowdy and downmarket. It was almost impossible to buy decent clothes. The gentlefolk of the neighbourhood, who typically were thrifty and impoverished, were no doubt equally disappointing as customers. Yet some shopkeepers were irritatingly complacent, even impertinent, prompting, at least on one occasion, a firm rebuke. Squire Chute of the Vyne, in town to settle his coal bill, complained to his supplier about the excessive prices. 'Well sir,' the man replied, 'you must remember that coals *is* coals, in these times.' 'I am glad to hear you say so,' riposted Chute, 'for what you have sent me lately have been mostly slates.' John Wesley, preaching here in 1759, had likened the inhabitants to 'the wild beasts at Ephesus … slow of heart and dull of understanding'.

## IV. Aunt Peggy's Lament
### 1. An Accumulation of Rats' Tails

It is 1856, and the 21-year-old Thomas Burberry, walking across the Market Place towards his new shop on the High Street, glances disapprovingly to his left. In the warm summer weather, his fellow tradesmen have gathered under the covered gateway of the Angel Inn, as is their wont, to smoke, drink and gossip.

The picturesque gateway, which on Oak Apple Day is festooned with oak boughs, leads into a spacious yard, where there are the usual stables, coach-houses and harness-rooms. There is even a disused ballroom, on the upper floor of one of the outhouses. Not long ago, the Angel was the principal coaching inn of Basingstoke, but most of its former business has been lost to the railways. It now advertises itself as a 'family hotel, tavern and commercial inn', and assures 'the Nobility, Gentry, Travellers by Railway, Commercial Gentlemen & others' that they will 'meet with every accommodation'. Post horses and all types of conveyance can be hired from here, even 'a well appointed hearse and mourning coaches'. Symbolic of its degradation, the original oak panelling in the parlour has long ago been hidden under canvas sheets which, in their turn, have been papered over. Now the shabby Angel can hardly claim even to be first among Basingstoke's many inns.

The society attracted to it consists mostly of idle shopkeepers, except for the periodic 'Visitation of the Clergy', when it swarms with clergymen in their black cassocks and the oak boughs are brought out again. The wide arch of the gateway is a convenient place to hang the venison that is served to the guests. It also has seating on both sides. In warm weather, the tradesmen are inclined to sit here all day, smoking their long clay pipes and drinking ale out of pewter pots, which they set down on the bench beside them. Dozens of them have their shops nearby, with pairs of steps leading up to them, and bay windows fitted with small panes of glass. Burberry passes a whole row of them on his left, including those of Adnams the grocer and Peskett the saddler. They occupy the former Maidenhead Inn - Peskett's premises are in the filled-in former archway - which is unrecognisable either as a coaching-inn or as the once-grand town-house of the Kingsmill family.

There are not so many customers that the proprietors cannot escape for long periods, leaving the shop boy in charge. Occasionally a boy will come to the Angel in search of his master. 'Please sir, Squire So-and-So wants to see you,' he will say, at which the tradesman will reluctantly lay down his pipe and shuffle back to his shop. A few, perhaps, are more business-like. Vanner and Johnson, whose drapery establishment adjoins the Angel on the east (the London Street) side, have installed plate-glass windows, the first in the town. Far into the future, the site will be converted into a McDonald's restaurant. How many of its customers, munching their hamburgers, will reflect on its significance?

The High Street is made up of the same timber-framed buildings that so disappointed Cosimo de' Medici when he visited in 1669. There is a ramshackle pub on London Street - past the 'twittern', or narrow covered walkway, leading to Caston's Foundry - called the Fleur-de-Lys (the regulars stubbornly refer to it as the 'Flower-de-Luce'), where Cromwell is reputed to have lodged before the storming of Basing House. The prisoners taken there were bound to the long wooden staples in its panelled entrance passage (though their commander, Lord Winchester, was held separately across the road, in the cellars of the Bell). According to legend, workmen digging the Basingstoke Canal in 1792 had discovered, in the ramparts at Basing, a rich haul of buried treasure. The mysterious Swiss watchmaker Roncoroni, whose shop is two doors down from the Fleur-de-Lys, is supposed to have bought a considerable part of it. There is a blacksmith's shop in between and the horses are shod in the street outside. The age of the train having dawned, traffic is minimal and the presence of the forge causes little disruption.

Burberry looks upon these buildings with a critical, unsentimental eye. To a forward-thinking Victorian, they have outlived their usefulness. A more encouraging sight is that of the Town Hall, built in 1832 on the north side of the Market Place, facing the Angel. Never mind that an entire row of attractive buildings had to make way for it, including the Royal Oak (on the corner of Church Street), the house of Mr Wallis with its two prominent bay windows on the ground floor and its weather vane, and that of Mr Caston, who had already shifted his ironmongery to the farther side of the square. The Town Hall of 1657, demolished at the same time, was a building of distinction, the finest in Basingstoke, yet considered an obstruction, as it intruded into the west side of the Market Place. The celebrated authoress, Jane Austen, who attended balls in its grand Assembly Rooms, dancing twenty dances in a night without fatigue, would surely have mourned its loss. The new one is similar enough - suspended on pillars, with an open market-hall beneath - but stands for modernity rather than the 'backwardness' of past ages. Even to the thrifty Burberry, the seemingly pointless reincarnation of the Town Hall, in so pedestrian a form, seems like £10,000 thoroughly well spent.

On the northern outskirts of the town, there are further encouraging signs of 'progress'. Joseph Locke's railway line from Nine Elms in Battersea (extended in 1848 to the new Waterloo Station) reached Basingstoke in 1839. With Brunel as chief engineer, the rival Great Western Railway added the line to Reading in 1848, with a stop at Mortimer. Queen Victoria herself was one of the first to use it. The separate halts for each company - one could hardly speak of a 'station' - were planted in green fields beside an old farmhouse and are surrounded by a low wall. The London and South Western Railway have provided a refreshment room that offers sandwiches, cold fowl, lemonade etc. - unspeakable fare, even if served by 'civil, efficient waiters'. An approach road - Station Hill - has been cut through the fields, but it is a lonely spot, a gathering place for the idle youth. An omnibus conveys rail passengers to and from the Angel, still hopeful for a share of the travelling trade.

The trains are a marvellous novelty, and it is worth visiting the station just to see them passing through. There are six a day to London, and the through trains to and from Southampton that roar past Basingstoke without stopping. The locomotives achieve speeds of over fifty miles per hour, faster than any man has ever travelled, though the difficult approach from Winchester tends to slow them down. Passengers are segregated into different 'classes', those in the third 'class' being consigned to open wooden carriages that have no seats and are better suited to goods or cattle. They struggle to maintain their balance and their dignity; and when it rains, huddle miserably under their umbrellas. Some have the added discomfort of smarting hands. As the incoming trains creep through the parish of Steventon, the passengers are offered bunches of wild flowers by agile boys with mischievous smiles, discovering as they grab them that the flowers are mixed with thistles.

The coming of the railways has been the most significant and exciting event in Basingstoke's history. The trains made it possible for millions of ordinary people to visit the Great Exhibition in the summer of 1851. Braving the open carriages, parties from Basingstoke were conveyed to London and back in a day, an extravagant outing but a wonderful experience for those who had never ventured far from the town. The Great Exhibition was contained in the vast 'Crystal Palace' in Hyde Park, and that was amazing enough, an unprecedented feat of engineering, a structure that was all steel and glass - and it was possible to imagine that even in Basingstoke there might, one day, be such buildings. The railways have made far-away places seem almost within reach. In 1854, a regiment was seen off from here on their way to the Crimea, after parading in the Market Place in their scarlet swallow-tailed coats and bearskins with brass chin-straps, few of them destined to return. Keen to exploit the potential of the railways, Arthur Wallis and Charles Haslam, successors to Caston's business, are even now raising the North Hants Ironworks at the bottom of Station Hill, with a view to increasing the production of their agricultural machinery and of penetrating ever more distant markets. They are helping to transform Basingstoke from a quiet market town into a centre of industry.

For now, apart from May's Brewery, established in 1750 on Chapel Hill, there is little development north of the river, which has to be forded at the bottom of Church Street. The wooden footbridge is regularly submerged, but strong men are willing to carry people across for a penny. Rustic Brook Street, flanked by a muddy ditch and ancient willows, is particularly damp. The Mays, who are farmers as well as brewers, work the land on the north side of the street, part of the Glebe Farm. There are some cottages at the bottom of Station Hill, one with a hornbeam tree in its garden, a disused silk mill and a further row of cottages on Noah's Island, which is completely encircled by the Loddon. When the stream overflows, its waters spread almost as far as the Barge Inn on Wote Street, then just as suddenly subside, leaving a carpet of weeds on the road. The way to Basing is aptly known as Water Lane.

It is incredible to think that Brook Street may one day be blasted out of existence and buried under a vast concrete platform. Will it astonish people in the 21$^{st}$ century, especially those shopping overhead, to learn that there were cottages with country gardens in the middle of the town, even a few with thatched roofs in Potter's Lane, and an untidy farmyard, that of Merton Farm, occupying almost the entire south side of Brook Street, as far as the junction with Wote Street? Cattle are apt to spill out of it and even to stray into nearby shops and pubs, but beasts are a common sight in all parts of the town, especially those being driven to the market on Wednesdays, or on their way to slaughter behind the butchers' shops (industrial abattoirs in out-of-the-way places are a shockingly cruel idea) - and it is with good reason that Cross Street, originally Cow Cross Lane, is so named.

Farmer Edmund Portsmouth, the tenant of Merton College, Oxford, lives in the large, whitewashed farmhouse by the ford at the bottom of Church Street, across the road from the Parsonage. It is only a short walk to his fields, which mainly lie between the Kingsclere and Aldermaston roads. On his way up Chapel Hill or 'Whiteway', a rough old road cut out of the chalky down, he passes rows of cramped but picturesque cottages. There are larks hanging in cages by almost every door, which delightfully erupt into choruses of song. The Aldermaston road, known locally as the Sherborne Road, is a narrow track, typical of the roads hereabouts. Bells hung from the collars of the leading horses forewarn of approaching vehicles. In the general stillness of the countryside, they can be heard for miles around.

There are four tollgates at strategic points around the town (there is one at the top of Chapel Hill, another in Duke Street, the country road leading to what was once the Duke of Bolton's estate at Hackwood), but the turnpike companies are failing businesses, with neither the means nor the inclination to maintain the roads. Steam-rollers and mechanical crushers are for the future. The best hope is that the larger stones will be kicked aside or ground down by the dwindling traffic, which, as a result, tends to throw up great clouds of white dust in dry weather. The local farmers are the main users, driving their waggons to the market or perhaps to the barn behind the church with loads of barley for malting. They occasionally employ impoverished old folk, men and women armed with hooked sticks, to collect the larger stones and to break them up with long-handled knapping hammers. It is skilled work but it takes them several days to work through each pile. With their protective wire-mesh goggles, these veterans can be an alarming sight. Intrepid riders of 'penny farthings' know that they must keep clear of the country roads when repairs are being carried out.

At Merton Farmhouse, Portsmouth has the enjoyment of a large, pleasant, walled garden. The river runs through it, minnows darting over its pebbly bed. The surface rainwater used to flow down the streets in torrents, causing it to flood the nearby houses in Church Street. A barrel drain, installed in 1837, prevents the regular cascades of mucky water, though they are still channelled into the Loddon at the bottom of Skew Lane (the future New Street), and selfish townsfolk are inclined to empty their water closets into the drain, rather than their own cesspits. As the pipe-smoking Portsmouth gazes pensively into the stream, there is small hope of its waters being fragrant and unpolluted, any more than there is of a quiet night at the Self Defence, the rowdy pub, favoured by gypsies, that is his near neighbour on the opposite bank.

The effects of water erosion are all too evident in 'Wote' or Oat Street, the route taken by carters bringing samples of corn from the farms for sale in the corn exchange under the Town Hall. On their way up the hill to the Market Place, they advertise their loads of oats, 'wutts' in the local dialect. Rough and narrow, Wote Street has no pavement - only a deep, smelly ditch on one side. Little wooden bridges lead to the adjacent houses and shops. There are steps leading down to the bar of the Cross Keys, the tiny old pub on the corner of Potter's Lane, next to Whiting the butcher's shop, which is a full yard below the present level of the street. The Feathers, at the top of the hill, is a more respectable establishment, an old coaching inn, but Wote Street is hard going for any sort of vehicle, and will remain so until the age of the motor-car. A few steps from the Cross Keys, just before Little Lane, are the premises of Jeremiah Watson, a millwright. Within fifty years, his son Frederick will have re-established himself, on the same site, as a cycle and motor engineer. Frederick and his wife will be photographed, on an outing to Stonehenge, in a Léon Bollée 3hp *voiturette*. Later still, Watson and Son will be subsumed under Festival Place.

The paving and lighting of the streets of Basingstoke, enabled by an Act of Parliament in 1815, has been a ponderous process. The first stones to be laid, at the top of Skew Lane, were pushed up again by giant mushrooms. There are foot-pavements in the High Street and Church Street and a few other parts of town. Street-lighting was delayed until 1834, when the gas works were opened between the Basing and Reading roads. The fish-tail gas jets on the main streets (the gas lamp-standard in the Market Place is particularly tall) are lit at dusk by the lamplighters using two-piece tubular rods and burners. The better-off homes are gas-lit and some even have gas cookers, but most people rely on the traditional tallow candles or even rush-dips. Both are manufactured by George Franklin, the grocer and tallow chandler, at the rear of his shop in Church Street. The periodic stench of the melting tallow is a necessary but singularly unpleasant aspect of life in the town.

Most people have also to contend with a joyless routine, dependent as they are on curmudgeonly masters and expected to work from 7 in the morning till 8 in the evening, with public holidays only on Oak Apple Day (29 May) and Christmas Day. The Sunday opening of many shops, a practice deplored by Burberry, affects the turnout at St Michael's Church. The ancient building is unheated and lit only by candles (they are placed in sockets in the pews, and the worshippers have to light them themselves), so evening services are unthinkable in winter. The experience is, in any case, somewhat dispiriting, with the psalms monotonously intoned rather than sung. There is no collection, most people having nothing to give. Mr Blunden, the aged clerk, sits at the front, with the choir in the gallery. The girls are to the fore in their red capes and straw hats, the boys behind, their singing accompanied by tuneless amateur musicians on bass viol and bassoon. Squire Apletree of Goldings, master of 1,000 acres, breezes in with his wife and his manservant, George White, who carries his books. Mrs Apletree, leading the way upstairs to their pew in the south gallery, is an impressive sight in her crinoline, which seems to fill the stairs. The Corporation, ever mindful of their dignity, also have their own pews, belatedly installed in 1836, but it is the resident farmers and their workers who stand out, each in his clean, white, Sunday smock, a familiar garment to the countryman Burberry, who is intrigued by its resistance to wind and rain.

Old Vicar Blatch - short, frail, clean-shaven - mounts the two-decker pulpit with difficulty. His removal of church furniture to Basing, part of the same living, has made him unpopular in certain quarters; yet he loves the poor, to whom he gives largely of his substance. As he staggers about the town on his stick, he always has a ready coin for a passing child. Unscrupulous boys are known to dash round corners, meet him again on the other side and thus receive a second bounty. Sometimes, on a whim, he calls at Mary Curtis's bakery and cake shop at 65 Church Street, buys up her entire stock of cakes and sweets and distributes them among the children outside. A fortunate few attend the Bluecoat Charity School in Cross Street, and assist with the Sunday School, which for most of the others - there are swarms of rough, unruly children in Basingstoke - will be their only form of schooling. Before lessons they are catechised around the font. Blatch regularly sets off in his phaeton to Basing and Up Nately, driven by Collier the coachman, to conduct services there. Mr Yeadon, his younger curate, helpmate and faithful companion, a fellow bachelor, will serve him for 37 years and outlive him by a matter of months, as if broken-hearted by his loss.

Mr Blatch is especially generous on fair days, when a boy doffing his cap or a girl curtseying might be rewarded with sixpence. The July sheep fair, held on the 'Fair Fields', is poorly attended, but the Michaelmas Fair Days are occasions of high excitement, a relief to the usual monotony. There is a great gathering of farm workers in the Market Place, all hoping to be hired or re-hired for the coming year. Each wears a distinctive badge in his hat to signify his particular skill or trade - straw for the ploughmen, whipcord for the carters and grooms, wool for the shepherds and hairs from a cow's tail for the cowmen. Various parts of the town are given over to the fair, including the meadow behind the Wheatsheaf and parts of Mr Portsmouth's garden at Merton Farm. There are swings and shooting galleries, boxing booths and horror shows, all of which tempt Blatch's protégés to part with their fairing coppers. There might even be gross exhibitions of a kind remembered from 1843, when George Ford, the noted rat-catcher, displayed the past seven years accumulation of rats' tails on the back of a waggon, a disgusting 43 bushels of them.

Delightful to the juveniles, the Michaelmas Fair is patiently endured by many of their elders, who quickly tire of the milling crowds and the incessant blast of the showman's organ. While the country people make the most of their holiday, the townsfolk are obliged to press on with their work. Only in the evening are they free to mingle with them in the various fairgrounds, a clay pipe hanging from every lip. With the pubs open all day, there is inevitably a good deal of drunkenness on the part of the visitors, who are given to shouting and occasionally brawling in the streets. Admittedly, the fair is good for business. The drapers' shops hold Michaelmas sales, encouraging the rustics to buy new jackets, trousers, boots etc. Even the disapproving Burberry sees the advantage of offering discounts on his speciality country clothing, though he knows better than to extend any credit.

Drunkenness, fighting and swearing are, in any case, established forms of release for the mass of the population who battle with poverty, overwork and boredom. There is little by way of wholesome distraction or entertainment. Theatrical performances by travelling companies, penny readings and 'spelling bees' are not to everyone's taste. The opportunities to skate by torchlight at Hackwood are memorable but rare. In the view of a respectable young townsman, Basingstoke is 'as near lifeless as it could be', without even the diversion of a local newspaper, and is not helped by the 'dry bones' on the Council. The seemingly innocuous Club days, and even cricket matches, are tediously prone to ending in violent disorder. Election days are occasions for joyous rioting, in anticipation of which the shopkeepers will already have put up their shutters. The smell of the malt in May's vats hangs over the town, a reminder that malting and brewing are important industries there, but its small population, barely exceeding 4,000, is served by no less than 31 inns and taverns and a further 20 beer-houses. Supper is rarely available at these places, apart from the occasional 'leg of mutton with all the trimmings'. Hard-drinking is condoned, even encouraged by the breweries, and the ill-concealed streak of evil in the town's low-life all too easily brought to the surface.

The respectable elements in Basingstoke - the industrious tradesmen, the Aldermen, the churchwardens, the earnest sectarians and other gentlemen in stove-pipe hats, assisted by some notoriously fat policemen - legislate ineffectually against minor disorders, but fail to address the heart of the problem. In the near future, terrible battles will be fought between Drink and Temperance; there will be a struggle for the soul of the Angel Hotel, that quasi-respectable haunt of idle sots, with Salvation Army banners held aloft and Burberry himself, the committed Christian and teetotaller, in the vanguard.

For now, a curious list of bye-laws is posted in prominent positions throughout the town. The first prohibits the use of dogs as beasts of burden or for the drawing of any 'cart, truck, barrow or other carriage'. The sight of dogs performing such roles was common enough before 1840! The second threatens heavy fines to those who wantonly knock on doors or ring their bells without lawful excuse, a favourite activity among naughty boys, who are much given to practical jokes. Indecent exposure of the person is quite properly proscribed, but the opposition of the town fathers to the use of 'any slide upon ice or snow', and to the driving and trundling through the streets of any hoop, suggests that they frown even on innocent fun.

The name appended to the 'Basingstoke Bye Laws' is that of Joseph Charles Shebbeare, Town Clerk, whose house, a particularly fine one, is at the bottom of Church Street, opposite the churchyard. Shebbeare is an attorney of rare dynamism and one of Basingstoke's ruling élite. His father Charles, a one-time 'Chymist and Druggist' in the town, had later practised with his own father, Joseph, as a surgeon in Odiham, from 68 High Street. Doubling as an attorney, Charles Shebbeare had also been the government agent responsible for the billeting on Odiham of large numbers of French prisoners-of-war. The Shebbeares are powerfully connected in Basingstoke, old Joseph having married Elizabeth May, one of the brewing Mays of Brook Street, from whom spring a regular supply of influential burgesses, aldermen and mayors.

Articled in 1808 to John Smallpiece of Guildford, Joseph Charles has been settled in the house on Church Street, once his father's, for over 25 years. Looking onto Church Square, it is surrounded by historic buildings of various sizes, including a large, jettied house on the opposite corner (which as early as 1575, when occupied by the Reeve family, had twenty rooms, including lofts). Shebbeare's house is hemmed between a row of houses on the north side - the nearest one, recorded since 1487, was home to the previous generation of Castons - and the impressively-porticoed Bedford House (formerly 'Tawkes' or 'Watermartens') on the south. Bedford House and Shebbeare's are separated by Little Lane, the long, narrow footpath connecting Church Street with Wote Street.

The core of Shebbeare's house, with its tall chimneys and uneven, tiled roof, is likewise timber-framed and dates from Tudor times. An 18th-century owner added corridors to the front and rear, shifting the staircase to the right of the oak-panelled hall. Shebbeare, who acquired the freehold in 1844, added substantial wings to the front, each the thickness of a room, to accommodate his busy offices. He installed a portico, and large sash-windows throughout, and encased the building in bright red brick. Whereas the original house had been set back from the road, the new wings extended it to the pavement. Despite the advanced growth of Virginia creeper, the exposed brickwork of Shebbeare's house glows the colour of flame in the evening sun. It is undoubtedly one of the finest houses in Basingstoke and a rival to the neighbouring Bedford House, which is currently occupied by Charles Penton. In later years, when it will be considered necessary to call it something other than 'Shebbeare's House', it will be known first as Ivy House, and then, somewhat misleadingly, as Queen Anne House.

The 'elected' Town Clerk since 1836 (much to the annoyance of the rival attorney George Lamb), Shebbeare is also Clerk to the Borough Magistrates and Registrar to the County Court, agent for the Royal Exchange Insurance Company and Coroner for the northern division of the County, commendably active for a man born in the year of the storming of the Bastille. It was typical of him that in 1852, elderly widower that he was, he should acquire a pretty second wife, Peggy, who is 33 years his junior. She no doubt takes great pleasure in the large garden or 'pasture' at the back of the house, over an acre of land extending northwards to the banks of the River Loddon and eastwards to Wote Street.[8] The high boundary wall that stretches as far as the Barge Inn leans perilously over that part of Wote Street, which is far from any street light and, at night-time, a place of terror. Few people care to pass that way alone and it is best negotiated with the aid of a lamp of horn or glass.

The garden, by contrast, is peaceful and pleasant, an appropriate haven for such a gentle soul. Peggy Shebbeare is fated to a life of blameless obscurity and quiet self-sacrifice, though her name is already honoured beyond the seas, and her fame in distant places will long outlive her.

[8] It was known variously as 'Holloway's' and 'Frogmede', which recalls the 'Toad Ford' of the medieval Caston family.

# 2. Kangaroo-tail Soup

John Garrett Bussell was the eldest of nine children of the Rev. William Marchant Bussell, Perpetual Curate of St Mary's, Portsea, and his wife Frances Louisa, known as Fanny. He was born at Portsea on 11 August 1802, within a year of his parents' wedding at St Mary's. William was from Devon but his wife, though born in the parish, had an altogether more exotic past. Her father, Thomas Legal Yates, was a Jamaican, probably descended from Edward Yates, a victualler of Port Royal, who died in 1677. Thomas had been sent to sea at the age of only eight, serving in H.M.S. *Centaur* at the siege of Havana. He had later acted as servant to his uncle, the surgeon Thomas Weir, in H.M.S. *Preston*. Another uncle, Captain Julian Legge, had commanded the 64-gun ship-of-the-line H.M.S. *Trident*, part of the fleet which, in 1759, had escorted Wolfe's army to Quebec. There was also a Mrs Yates of Port Royal, perhaps Thomas's mother, who in 1780 had nursed the ailing Nelson, being at that time housekeeper to Lady Parker, the wife of the naval commander-in-chief.

Thomas and his younger brother Nick had both become pursers in the navy and had later retired to England, where Thomas was employed as a prize agent. They had married the two daughters of another distinguished Jamaican, Ballard Beckford, whose fabulously rich relatives, with vast sugar estates on the island, included William Beckford, the eccentric creator both of Fonthill House, a magnificent Gothic folly in Wiltshire, and of *Vathek*, a sublimely-crafted Gothic novel. The Yateses, however, were far from wealthy, despite their business interests and property in Jamaica, which included a 'depreciating' 420-acre plantation called Prospect Hill.

Money being tight, the premature death of William Marchant Bussell, in 1820, was a disaster for his young family, but Fanny came from redoubtable stock and was determined to cope. Bussell had provided an endowment policy for each child; friends and relations clubbed together to raise a further £3,000 and invest it on their behalf. John was at that time a foundation scholar in his last year at Winchester College, intended for Oxford and the Church. William was to be a surgeon and Lenox a sailor. A place was found for their clever, 9-year-old brother Charles at Christ's Hospital, the famous charity school in the City of London, whilst Vernon and Alfred, then aged 6 and 4 respectively, were in due course sent also to Winchester, though it was an horrendous den of vice and iniquity. The family had to move out of the vicarage at Portsea and for years were dependent on the hospitality of relatives, migrating between their houses in various parts of the country.

John unexpectedly failed to secure a close scholarship to New College, the school's sister foundation, so went instead, as an exhibitioner, to Trinity. His tutors loved him and awarded a second exhibition. Further support arrived from an unexpected source. Having been savagely bullied by his fagmaster at Winchester, John had vowed, if ever he became a prefect, to treat his own fag with kindness. The fortunate boy was devoted to John and pursued him to Oxford, whence his guardian had to retrieve him. In gratitude, she settled an additional £100 a year on John for his remaining time at the university.

John hoped that his graduation, in the Trinity term of 1829, would be swiftly followed by his ordination, but the Bishop of Salisbury informed him that he would not be ordaining again until 11 October. He took a temporary job as tutor to the sons of John Willis Fleming, M.P., of North Stoneham Park, near Southampton, migrated with them to Binstead House, their seat on the Isle of Wight, and was introduced that summer to the Molloys, a couple on their honeymoon. Captain John Molloy of the Rifle Brigade and his much younger bride, the former Georgiana Kennedy from Carlisle, were a good match, both being restless idealists. They talked of their intention to settle, within the year, in Western Australia, where a new colony was to be founded. Coincidentally, the same idea had already occurred to at least one of the Bussells.

Charles Bussell was the tallest and strongest of the brothers, but suffered from an appalling stammer, a terrible social handicap and one that precluded him from any sort of professional career. 'I have scarcely entered a house without some person or other laughing in my face,' Charles wrote, and 'am literally sighing for the greenwood shade'. The family were receiving favourable reports from a friend, Lieutenant Spicer, who had charge of 70 convicts in New South Wales. He described a pleasant country that was stocked with an abundance of game, including kangaroos. Above all, it was cheap: '£100 will go as far as £500 in England,' he wrote. The chief drawback was its villainous population. The 'bushrangers' being desperate men, it was 'dangerous to go out of sight of the town, day or night'.

A scheme had been announced, however, for a new, convict-free colony in Western Australia, in the virtually-unexplored Swan River District. On 18 June 1829, Captain James Stirling, R.N., had called for settlers, promising free grants of land in an area 'not inferior to the plains of Lombardy'. Each could expect to receive 40 acres of land for every £3 invested in stock and equipment. Like the Molloys, Charles, Vernon and Alfred were all enthused by the prospect, and Fanny Bussell, realising that it was a way to secure the future of the whole family, prevailed upon John to give up his idea of ordination and lead them out there with the first party. The benevolent Mr Fleming and the family's chief trustee, Captain Robert Yates, R.N. - Fanny's 'Cousin Bob' - were fully in favour of the plan.

John, Charles, Vernon and Alfred Bussell - aged 26, 19, 16 and 14 - their servant, Pearce, and other passengers including the Molloys, embarked on the *Warrior* at Portsmouth on 9 October 1829. The brothers had goods and chattels entitling them to a land grant of some 5,500 acres, but travelled steerage to save money, supplying their own bedding and provisions. Banned from going 'abaft the mainmast', they had to put up with decks leaking 'with the effusion of swine and cattle'. Various comforts had been provided by the Whicher family of Petersfield, generous and supportive cousins on their mother's side, who must have sent them down to the *Warrior* while she was loading, Petersfield being only 16 miles inland from Portsmouth. 'The hams and preserves were excellent,' they reported to Fanny from the Cape. 'In fact, everything is, so that you must not fail to thank again the Petersfield friends.' Charles writes to their brother William: 'almost everything which your providence supplied he will find very grateful, but I think nothing more so than the gingerbread sent from our friends at Petersfield. The pickles we have found super ...' Characteristically, the fearless John was quick to adopt 'the main-top as a refuge from eternal noise and foul savours'. The four-and-a-half-month voyage was an early test of their endurance.

The *Warrior* arrived at Fremantle on 12 March 1830. The Bussells presented Stirling with a letter of introduction from 'Cousin Bob', his old shipmate; but found that all the good land around Fremantle and Perth had already been 'pegged out'. On Stirling's advice, the brothers set out in May for Cape Leeuwin, 200 miles to the south, with a view to founding a sub-colony there. Their 30-strong party comprised three families - the Bussells and Molloys, who constituted 'the gentle settlers', and the 'cockney' Turners - along with some labourers and sailors. They established themselves first at the port of Augusta, at the mouth of the Blackwood River, lived in tents whilst constructing houses with thick rubble walls and thatched roofs, and set about clearing the land. 'The land is fertile,' John informed his mother; 'the grand difficulty is clearing away trees of stupendous magnitude and great hardness.' When the day's work was done, he consoled himself with Paley's *Moral Philosophy*.

Soon they abandoned the port and headed twelve miles up-river, to an area that was no less densely wooded. On the 'Adelphi' peninsula, named in honour of the brothers, they put in six hours a day to the common task of clearance, after which each man was free to work on his own hut. Here, too, they met with defeat. A handful of men would never prevail against a primeval forest, where trees with trunks up to 38 feet in circumference rose tall and straight into the sky. They had to dig their meagre field with spades in a futile attempt at wheat-growing. Their cattle regularly strayed and were lost. John complained besides that he was short of money: 'Molloy has taken my servant off our hands, so that one drain on our provisions is removed'.

John turned into a fearless explorer, setting out on foot for extended periods. In December 1831, he ranged to a region sixty miles north of Augusta, on the south side of Geographe Bay. It was called 'the Vasse' - the hapless Thomas Vasse, botanist on a French ship, the *Geographe,* having vanished there twenty years before, while searching for specimens; speared to death, no doubt, by angry natives. This was a country of fine natural pastures, gigantic trees (save the odd tuart) being reassuringly absent. John persuaded the Augusta settlers to transfer there *en masse.* They were joined for the undertaking, in January 1833, by John's brother Lenox and his sisters Frances and Bessie, who found John in possession of a full beard, such as an older man might wear, though it was 'beautifully combed'. He had vowed to keep it until their 'Little Mama' came out. The girls observed him skinning his first kangaroo, during which he recited appropriate passages from the *Georgics.* He kept a well-stocked library in his hut, where Byron and Gibbon jostled with classical authors. The girls voiced mild complaints about the dust and fleas.

Their mother sent the family silver ahead of her, but it was lost in the wreck of the *Cumberland* on its way to Augusta. 'I had set up my mind for a silver fork,' Alfred told her, 'but never mind, a steel one is very good when a person is hungry.' The settlers were transferred to the Vasse in the *Ellen* in April 1834, with all their remaining goods. The enraged Aborigines were placated by having a gun pointed at them, upon which they became friendly, shaking hands with the newcomers and directing them to the nearest well.

That winter, they lived mainly on fish, 'fat hen' (a disgusting vegetable) and native spinach, and 'the boys were constantly sick after their meal'. Then one of their stray cows, originally bought from a Mr Yule and named 'Yulika', miraculously re-appeared, having been missing for months. She was to be a great asset (and was soon to calve in the bush, producing the bull 'Hudson'). In Yulika's honour, the new Bussell homestead was named 'Cattle Chosen'. 'Little Mama', with her daughters Mary and Fanny, having landed in Geographe Bay on 19 January 1835, were escorted there amid great rejoicing.

The house the brothers had built with their own hands was by then a 'comfortable, substantial-looking mansion. It is white, and the four upper windows in the upper storey give it a cheerful and finished look, which perhaps it does not quite deserve. As you approach it the garden, well fenced and productive in all English vegetables, would almost make you forget that you are in Australia. The piano occupies its place under the window … The windows command on one side a pleasant view of the river, with the country in its unredeemed state.'

With the Molloys and others soon settled nearby, Governor Stirling was delighted. The brothers marked out the site of a small port, which in 1835 was officially named 'Busselton'. Bessie describes the Vasse as 'a beautifully undulating grassy lawn, between the huge tooart trees', where the kangaroos are 'seen in herds, which accounts for the natives being so numerous'. Accustomed to spearing any animal that passed their way, the Aborigines were no respecters of the white man's cattle, and considered themselves free to beset and pilfer his property. As far as the British government was concerned, they were equal subjects under the law. Violence against them was forbidden. John was repelled by their habits and 'revolting laugh', but felt he should treat them kindly and provide for them. They called him 'Mitter Buttle' or 'Mowen', were grateful for his rations, and were to preserve a fond memory of him.

5 feet 6 inches tall, with brown hair and blue eyes, John Garrett Bussell was a man of remarkable courage and tenacity, a natural leader, whose pleasant voice and quiet humour inspired trust and confidence. The achievement of the early settlers, who successfully recreated the atmosphere of southern England amid the 'sandy wastes and flyblown savages', was considerable. The chief protagonists were the products of three of England's most famous public schools. Stirling had been to Westminster, Molloy to Harrow and the Bussell boys to Winchester. Molloy was a particularly interesting companion. Having transferred from the navy to the army, he had the distinction - perhaps unique - of fighting both at Trafalgar and Waterloo, where he was severely wounded. He was, moreover, the natural son (by the Countess of Tyrconnel) of Frederick, 'the grand old' Duke of York and Albany, second son of King George III. The Duke had combined being Lay Bishop of Osnabrück with command of the

British Army, his pointless manoeuvres inspiring the famous nursery rhyme. As Government Resident in Augusta in 1832, Molloy drew names for its streets and natural features from the titles of his late father, whom he closely resembled. There were Osnaburg Street, York Street, Albany Terrace, Duke's Head and Point Frederick. He must have had fascinating tales to tell, and Waterloo Day was always celebrated at Fairlawn, the Molloy homestead in the Vasse.

John Bussell may not have wanted for good company, but conspicuously lacked two essentials: money with which to continue his schemes, and a wife. He dreamed of installing a horse-drawn flour-mill, and of stocking his farm with imported English sheep. As for a wife, his prospects of finding one in Australia, already extremely limited, were further reduced by his discounting any woman who was not his social equal. It was in pursuit of these aims that he embarked in 1837 for England.

Staggering ashore after a long and harrowing journey, John at once resumed his courtship of Miss Sophy Hayward, his youthful sweetheart. An orphan, brought up in Bengal, Sophy was spoken of by 'Little Mama' as 'the fickle Indian', perhaps because she aspired to be mistress of her own house. Though formally engaged, their relationship was doomed. John wrote to his mother in March 1838, after taking legal advice, to inform her that his affair with Sophy was at an end. 'We have had nothing but differences since my arrival. I was estranged at first by foolish jealousy of my affections for you, and lastly I objected to the reversion of her property, once willed to me, being, now that I had come for her, settled upon her brother. I have encountered distracting and humiliating scenes, and bear with her silly friends the character of a fortune hunter.'

Marriage would have been as respectable a way of raising capital as any, yet John was thwarted at every turn: 'I can touch none of our funded property,' he wrote, 'so accurate and exact are the trustees, amongst whom Robert Yates appears the most timid. Our sheep affair still remains in doubt, there seems such fear among our enterprising sleeping partners.' He was similarly frustrated in his renewed quest for a wife.

On 3 May 1838, he sent a formal proposal, through her father, to his 15-year-old cousin, Margaret Whicher. Born on 21 May 1822, she was the eldest daughter of James Whicher, a Surgeon of Petersfield, Hampshire, and his wife Anna. They were the 'Petersfield friends' whose tasty morsels had sustained the Bussell brothers during their voyage to Australia, and had no doubt helped them in other ways, with financial support and hospitality in the hard times of their youth.

Anna Whicher was 'Little Mama's' cousin. Her mother was a Yates and her father, Thomas Weir from Dunmurry, County Antrim, was the naval surgeon who had taken Fanny's own father to sea. The Weirs' daughter Margaret, born in Port Royal, Jamaica, in 1769, had married Lieutenant-General Charles Norris Cookson, R.A., at that time commanding a company of gunners in the town. Margaret had died at Woolwich in 1807, after giving birth to her ninth child. Anna was the third of these children, born in Port Royal in 1792, and married to James Whicher since 1816. In 1820, her younger sister Mary had married 'Cousin Bob' Yates, the Bussells' truculent trustee, with whom she lived at Alverstoke.

Old General Cookson, meanwhile, had remarried in 1810 to John's aunt, Mary Bussell, and had retired with her to the Bussell family home, Kenton House in Devon, where he died in 1830. There were thus at least three intimate family connections that bound the Whichers with the Bussells. Moreover, Anna and Mary's brother, Joseph Yates Cookson, had preceded Charles Bussell to Christ's Hospital, the Cookson family no doubt influencing Charles's admission there.

The Whichers lived at no.12 High Street, Petersfield, which James, born at no.4 in 1788, had acquired by 1809, a year or two after qualifying as an M.R.C.P. His father and grandfather had also been doctors in the town. The house is documented since medieval times, and its exposed timbers, visible from a side passage, bespeak great age, but James had evidently prospered sufficiently to add imposing bay windows at the front. There was a long, narrow, walled garden at the rear, and space, under an archway, for a carriage. Nearby was a former coaching inn, The White Hart, whose famous guests had included Charles II, Peter the Great and Samuel Pepys.

Anna Whicher had given birth to eleven children in fifteen years. The surviving son, James, born in 1825, was to study medicine at St Andrews and would become a notably dashing naval surgeon - 'the Handsome Mate of the Med Fleet'. His beautiful sisters, famous throughout the town, were Margaret, Sophia, Rhoda, Alice, Mary and Laura, known as 'the Bewitchers'. All had been baptised in the parish church by their uncle John, the curate of Petersfield. Margaret, nicknamed 'Peggy', was a lively girl, whose passion for amateur dramatics was to land her in trouble. She persuaded her father to lend family portraits as props for a local production. A fire broke out in the theatre, and the precious heirlooms were destroyed. An extremely loving and dutiful daughter, she was no doubt soon forgiven.

John would only recently have become re-acquainted with Peggy, whom he last saw when she was six years old - and he twenty-six. As she had yet to turn sixteen, her father considered her far too young to marry, let alone cope with life in a 'wilderness'. James Whicher replied to John Bussell's proposal on 8 May, with a polite but firm refusal:

> *'To you my dear Bussell personally neither I nor Anna had any objection. It would on the contrary, under more auspicious circumstances, have given us happiness to have entrusted her to your protection. The only obstacle which might not perfectly have been got over is her extreme youth, her yet unformed mind & the impossibility of being able to count upon her firmness to carry her through the arduous adventure she would have essayed in case she had been left to the evident failings of her yet uninformed childhood, without the caution & guidance of her parents. The more I reflect the more I am convinced that the happiness of both of you has been best consulted by the decision I have come to.'*

The Whichers felt that John needed a more mature and experienced companion, and that Margaret would not thank them if, 'in her extreme youth, it had pleased God to leave her alone in your wilderness'. However, John should not give up all hope, for 'It may be otherwise hereafter than can at present be conjectured'.

Marriage to Margaret would have secured a useful settlement for John and her father's active support for his schemes. Intending that Whicher and Bob Yates should be the English 'backers' of his sheep-farming venture, he proposed, as a preliminary, that they sponsor the transportation to the new colony of much-needed labour. A cautious Whicher foresaw that these labourers, beneficiaries of 'a sort of gratis immigration', would immediately want to 'settle down upon their own 5 or 10 or 20 acres'. He suspects 'that this will be encouraged by your new Governor, and perhaps it may be his duty to do so', in which case their investment would have been for nothing. John was nevertheless politely encouraged, 'when your opportunities enable you, to give me information upon our points of interest'.

The mounting strain was too great even for John, who collapsed with a nervous breakdown. He went to recover in Plymouth with his aunt Elizabeth and her husband John Bowker, a naval captain who had once been governor of Newfoundland. Whicher continued to correspond with him in cordial terms, but assumed a frostier tone when, in late August, he heard of John's sudden marriage to Mrs Charlotte Cookworthy.

The sister of his old friend, Lieutenant Spicer, Charlotte was a widow with three small children. They lived in the city where the 'Plymouth Brethren' had, in recent years, held their first assemblies. The late Mr Cookworthy was a convert to the sect, and had appointed fellow members as his children's trustees and guardians. They strongly disapproved of Charlotte's engagement, within three weeks of their meeting, to the Anglican John, with whom she had even been seen in church.

Although it might have seemed to the Whichers and others that he had selected a new bride, and married her, with indecent haste, John had good cause for doing so. Threatened with the removal of her children, Charlotte had resolved on eloping with them to Australia, where they would be out of reach. Having embarked in the *Montreal* in Gravesend, the newly-weds persuaded the agents of the ship to have it anchor off Plymouth Hoe and, with the Bowkers' help, quietly spirited the children aboard.

Charlotte's inheritance from her husband was, of course, withheld, but a legacy of £600 from her mother more than compensated John for his expenses in England, which included purchases of improved plant and stock. They arrived at Cattle Chosen in May 1839.

With his various acquisitions, including a resolute and capable wife, John must have felt vindicated. He had also brought back the legal document detailing his arrangement with Whicher and Yates, who had agreed to finance his sheep-farming venture in return for a share of the profits. One of John's first tasks on his return was to assist the cartographer Arrowsmith in compiling a new map of the area, for that of 1838 was already out of date. Under John's guidance, wildernesses were helpfully labelled with terms such as 'Good land', 'Rocky and heavily timbered' or 'Kangaroo abundant'. What better way of complimenting his backers than to lend their names to prominent geographical features that were hitherto unnamed? Thus, in the terrain that he himself had been the first European to explore, he inserted a Whicher Range near the source of the Vasse River and a Mount Yates above the Blackwood. Above all, he honoured the child-bride who might have been in his naming of Margaret River, which, rising in the Whicher Range, flows into the Indian Ocean at a point midway between Cape Naturaliste and Cape Leeuwin. A modest tributary to Margaret River was named 'Mowen', John's own Aboriginal nickname, the only union there was ever to be between them. Whether he had felt any strong sentimental attachment to Margaret is unknown, as are her own views on the matter. It is nevertheless curious that none of the more prominent ladies of his family was ever to receive any sort of territorial recognition - not even Charlotte herself.

Sadly, John's sheep-farming dream was never realised, although, in 1840, both the Whichers and Yateses talked of joining him in Australia. 'Cousin Bob' Yates, a grizzled veteran who had lost an eye in action and was soon to lose the sight in his other eye, had eleven young children to support and faced an impoverished old age. John went so far as to prepare a home for him in the Vasse, but Yates never came. He held off transferring the Bussells' capital to Australia for as long as possible, and eventually did so after making heavy deductions, including interest on his own 'expenses'. It was not Bob who emigrated but his children - to Tasmania.

John's disappointment in business seems insignificant compared to his achievement in opening up that part of Australia. His greatest personal satisfaction was to have founded the little church of St Mary's, Busselton. It was modelled on the chapel of Winchester College, all the settlers near Busselton helping to quarry the stone or cart timber to the site. In this very English setting, wearing his old gown and hood of a Bachelor of Arts, John was personally to conduct services until his death in 1875, though he declined to be ordained - he was too attached to his role as a magistrate. For two years from 1862 he also taught Classics at Perth High School, and, in 1870, was nominated a member of the Western Australian Legislative Council. He had four daughters with Charlotte. Their descendants still live at Cattle Chosen.

There would be no return trips to England for John's brothers, whose choice of wives was severely restricted. In August 1850, at the age of 36, Alfred married Ellen Heppingstone, the daughter of a Scots couple who had been servants in the Molloy household. To escape the condescension of his family, Alfred headed south to the Margaret River, intent on carving out his own estate. In 1857, on a site where Nyungar Aborigines had been camping for thousands of years, he built the Ellensbrook Homestead. Around a framework of rough bush poles, with an old boat's mast as a ridge beam, he raised walls of crushed shells and limestone, finally sealing them with an improvised form of plaster. Here, with great force of will, he established a successful beef and dairy farm. He became as adept in bush medicine as in the Aboriginal dialect, and a great friend to the natives, upon whose labour he depended. He and Ellen had fourteen children, three of whom died in infancy. They left unhappy Ellensbrook in 1865, Alfred building an even finer residence, Wallcliffe House, in a stunning location near the mouth of the Margaret River.

Their daughter Grace, who ran wild about the estate, a fearless horsewoman and explorer of caves, became a 16-year-old celebrity in 1876, and is remembered as the 'Grace Darling of Western Australia'. While working in the kitchen at Wallcliffe, Grace heard that the S.S. *Georgette* had run aground in nearby Caldardup Bay. With her father's Aboriginal stockman, Sam Isaacs, she rushed to the scene. The pair repeatedly rode into the raging surf to pull the stricken passengers ashore, saving at least fifty lives. Grace was rewarded for this feat with the Royal Humane Society's Silver Medal, Sam having to make do with the Bronze.

Impressed by her story, an intrepid young surveyor, Frederick Drake-Brockman, rode 300 miles from Perth, determined to meet her. After their marriage at Busselton in 1882, Drake-Brockman became notable as an explorer of uncharted regions and for marking out the second line of the infamous Rabbit-Proof Fence. In 1915 he was appointed Surveyor-General of Australia. His middle child by Grace, Deborah Drake-Brockman, was 'an individualist from an early age'. She defied her parents by marrying, at Busselton in 1905, the newspaper proprietor Sir Winthrop Hackett, who was forty years her senior. Their son John, born in Perth in 1910, was educated at Geelong Grammar School and at New College, Oxford, returning, like his great-grandfather Alfred, to a Wykehamist foundation. Known as 'Shan', and with no hint of an Australian accent, Hackett was commissioned into the 8th King's Royal Irish Hussars and was much decorated during the Second World War. In 1944 he commanded the 4th Parachute Brigade for the assault on Arnhem. General Sir John Hackett, who in retirement became Principal of King's College, London, died in 1997, the distinguished offspring of a remarkable line.

As for Margaret Whicher, her opportunity for a life of adventure had passed. The family abandoned their plans to emigrate and, whilst her younger sisters collected husbands, it seemed that she was doomed to permanent spinsterhood. Her father proved far from averse to marrying his daughters to older men, even those likely to live abroad. The youngest girl, Laura, was married at sixteen to her 32-year-old cousin George Remington Cookson, a future Major-General in the Indian Army. The couple's voyage to India was unusually long, for they were becalmed in the Doldrums. George was then appointed Collector of Meerut, where the Mutiny erupted in 1857. Laura's loyal servants had to conceal her, with her baby, from a rampaging mob. Later, she stood with the English sergeant on the walls of the Dum Duma fort as the mutineers charged. Peggy was to lead a very quiet life in comparison.

It was on 25 November 1852, a little over a year after Laura's wedding, that Peggy's father at last led her to the altar in Petersfield Church. The bridegroom, Joseph Shebbeare, was an old fossil of 63, only a few months younger than James Whicher himself, but the son of a colleague in a neighbouring town. A widower whose only daughter, Marion, was three years older than Peggy, he was no doubt undemanding as regarded a settlement, being comfortably settled in Church Street, Basingstoke, a quaint old market town, much like Petersfield.

Shebbeare's house, later known as Queen Anne House, was to be Peggy's home for nearly fifty years. Joseph died there on 3 March 1860, leaving her his entire estate - only £600 in effects, but his house and other property in Basingstoke, cottages in Dummer and Preston Candover and a small farm in Silchester. Peggy soon abandoned Basingstoke, however, to care for her aged parents, a sacrifice that James Whicher acknowledged in January 1873 when writing his will. In recognition of her 'having broken up her home and establishment in Basingstoke and of her loss thereby in devoting her time for many years to the care of myself and her late mother', he left her all his furniture and possessions, half his house and lands and the equivalent of a year's rent at his final address. Anna Whicher had died at Petersfield in 1869. James had let out the house and retired, with Peggy as his carer, to Southsea. He died there on 18 April 1875, aged 87.

A year later, in London, the now-liberated Peggy married another widower, Samuel Chandler, her late husband's junior partner. Samuel's father of the same name, a bookseller, stationer and printer at 81 Winchester Street, was also a keen antiquarian and publisher of his own works on local history, such as *The History of Basing House*. A long-standing member of the Corporation, Samuel junior had been at the centre of an exciting event in March 1863, when the honeymooning Prince and Princess of Wales had passed through Basingstoke in the royal train. During its three-minute stop at the station, to change lines and take on water, Chandler and his fellow aldermen had presented their congratulations. They had previously posed for a photograph at Ramage's studio and were photographed again on the platform, looking extremely dignified in their stove-pipe hats. An enormous crowd had assembled, including an estimated 4,000 people from surrounding villages, to share in the excitement. The church bells rang, a band paraded the town and dinner for 2,000 was served under a tent in the Market Place. Chandler did his turn as Mayor in 1869-70 and died on 10 January 1885, aged 73. His children were Wills and Frank, both solicitors in Basingstoke, along with Richard, Margaret, Emily and Ada, the only daughter to marry.[9]

Peggy was no doubt on excellent terms with her step-children, two of the girls continuing to live with her after Samuel's death. They were still remembered in Basingstoke in 1966. With the bulldozers poised, the artist Diana Stanley made a wonderful final record of the house. She writes: 'These energetic ladies were interested in a number of activities, particularly in the Sunday School movement and, on one occasion, they organised a large tea-party for children from both Church and Chapel. They were all assembled inside the big gateway of Queen Anne House, or Chandlers as some then called it, where each child was given a ticket and a tin mug to tie around the neck. Late in life the two Chandler ladies took to cycling, which was very enterprising at a time when cycling was considered to be improper for ladies, especially as they were obliged to wear bloomers. To avoid attracting attention the two ladies rose very early in the morning and left the house by the back door. Pushing their bicycles up Chapel Street they soon gained the countryside and pedalled merrily away.'

By 1900 the ageing Peggy was living with her nephew, Arthur Peskett, his wife

---

9  Wills's son, Hugh Wills Chandler, practiced as a solicitor, first in Basingstoke and then in Fleet, until he was over 90. He died in 1954, having seemed to many to be 'the last survivor from Dickens's novels'.

Edith and their numerous children at 57 Brockley Road, New Cross. The Kentish village was at that time rapidly transforming into today's unlovely suburb. Arthur, the son of Peggy's sister Alice, had an easy commute to the London Hospital, where he was a House Surgeon. Peggy sold the Basingstoke house in 1901, and by 1904 had accompanied the Pesketts to 3 Clermont Road, Preston Park, Brighton. She died there on 22 March 1915, aged 92, leaving her entire estate to Arthur's elderly, unmarried sisters, Blanche and Laura. Arthur's eldest son Guy, the peace-time chartered accountant who registered the death, was to be reported missing in action in France in 1917, aged 26.

There have now been eight generations of Margarets in Peggy's family since Margaret Weir, the sister of Dr Thomas Weir. They include Peggy's great-grand-niece, the present writer's mother, whose middle name is Margaret. Peggy probably forgot all about the Australian river that had been named after her. She would have known nothing of the eponymous town that grew up at its mouth, a sleepy place at the time of her death, with no pub and a single hotel that doubled as a post office. With its Mediterranean climate, endless golden beaches and crashing surf, it was inevitable that it should develop later in the century into a 'chilled out surfie town'. Since the late-1960s, it has also been the centre of an internationally-renowned wine-growing region, whilst the coastline is world-famous for its surfing breaks and opportunities for whale- and dolphin-watching. The publishers of the *Lonely Planet* travel guides have rated it among the 'Top 10 Regions in the World', for, as half a million people discover each year, it is a place of wild beauty, the perfect destination for an adventurous, outdoor holiday - a world away from Basingstoke, in every sense.

# V. London SW50

'As a Hampshire - and Basingstoke - man, I can't help wondering just what the speech here will sound like in a few generations. Will Hampshire's country dialect survive? Or will Basingstoke become, through accent, "London SW50"?'

K.R. Dykes, *Hampshire Magazine,* May 1967

In the spring of 1944, there was considerable excitement in Basingstoke. One of the biggest stars of the day was in town to work on his latest film. *He Snoops to Conquer* was the seventh George Formby vehicle to be directed by Marcel Varnel. The pair were to collaborate on nine films in all and Formby played the same character in each of them - a gormless, accident-prone innocent with a cheeky grin and unvarnished Lancashire accent.

George Formby (who died in 1961 and presumably is now largely forgotten) had made his name as a performer of comic songs, to which he would often accompany himself on the 'banjolele'. Despite his frequent lapses into *double entendre,* Formby was too disarming to be truly shocking, though his 1937 number, 'With my little stick of Blackpool Rock', describing various inventive uses to which that object is put, had been banned by prudish officials at the B.B.C. Formby's winsome charm is encapsulated in his catch-phrases, including (an expression of surprise) 'Eeh! Well I'll go to our 'ouse' and the reassuring 'It's turned out nice again'. By the late 1930s such nonsense was earning him £100,000 a year.

Varnel, a French-born Old Carthusian, had earlier directed Will Hay in *Oh! Mr Porter,* one of the comic masterpieces of British cinema, which is often included in lists of the top one hundred films of all time. The railway station in *Oh! Mr Porter* is that at Cliddesden, which, during filming in the summer of 1937, had only recently been abandoned. Meanwhile, Varnel would have been able to assess the potential of nearby

Basingstoke for location filming. The town is ideally cast in *Snoops* as the fictional 'Tangleton', but the film is a disappointment, a workmanlike churning-out of a tired old formula, which marks the decline of Formby's popularity as a cinema actor. To the particular regret of his *aficionados,* he takes up his banjolele in only one of the three songs in *Snoops* - 'surely this is going too far!' A critical disaster, the film has never been shown since its initial screening, either in cinemas or on television, and might have disappeared entirely. In 2004, a rare print obtained by the George Formby Society became 'the pride' of its archives, and in 2009 a sparkling new edition, made from material preserved by the British Film Institute, was released on D.V.D., testimony to the enduring interest in Formby's work.

Honest, good-hearted, relentlessly cheerful - he even performed in the London Underground during the Blitz - Formby stood in wartime for the indomitable spirit of the British. In 1944 he was at the height of his popularity, attracting large crowds wherever he went. Formby and his co-stars stayed at the Red Lion Hotel in London Street, where their rooms were burgled (a private in the Royal Fusiliers was sentenced to nine months in prison for the crime), but generally they received a warm, sometimes wildly enthusiastic reception from the townsfolk. On the last day of filming, Formby addressed a large crowd from the Town Hall balcony to say his farewells, but the microphone failed to work and his voice was drowned out by the passing traffic. The electrician responsible is said to have been hounded out of town.

The chief interest of *He Snoops to Conquer* is now as a period piece of remarkable topicality. Formby plays George Gribble, an odd-job man for Tangleton Rural District Council. Some chain-smoking reporters arrive from London to enquire about 'the little people'. They want to know what the government is doing about post-war planning in a typical English town. Based on information that a naïve Gribble has provided, they run a front-page story that highlights the inequities in housing. Whilst four people occupy the mansion of one of the town councillors, fourteen are crammed into the tiny, terraced house where Gribble himself lodges.

In order to qualify for a government grant, the crafty councillors have the nearest available 'idiot', Gribble, conduct a 'Public Opinion Investigation', in the course of which he questions working men in flat caps and women with countless babies about their living conditions. They are almost overwhelmingly dissatisfied with their lot and with the ineffectiveness of the local administration. They complain of leaky roofs, rotten floorboards, collapsing plaster and the lack of a bathroom. One character is seen bathing in a tub in front of the fire. All the interiors look much like those from the Victorian era that are recreated in the Milestones Museum.

The corrupt bank manager Henry Oxbald has a grip on the Council. In their disregard for democracy, they are considered 'worse than the Nazis'. Oxbald instructs the unwitting Gribble to dispose of the unfavourable forms - the majority - which he puts out for salvage. The scandal is exposed when Gribble, struggling to control the roadsweeping van in which the papers have been collected, inadvertently scatters them in the streets. There is a shot of him hurtling round a corner into Church Square, a scene that is quite unrecognisable today. Queen Anne House can be seen in the background and a razed area opposite marks the site of the historic Reeve house, which had been flattened by a bomb in 1940. Lower Brook Street, which has also been comprehensively obliterated from the map, doubles for 'Paradise Row', the inaptly-named poor quarter of Tangleton in which Gribble himself resides, with leafy Eastrop Lane, a broad boulevard lined with capacious 1930s villas, representing the affluent end of the town.

*Snoops* is undisguised political propaganda from a time when the end of the war was in sight. It captures the mood of a nation that, in July 1945, was to return the Labour Party to power with a massive majority. The heartless 'toffs' who run Tangleton are blatant caricatures. They oppose a re-development plan because it involves the demolition of Paradise Row, from which many of them draw rents, and the replacement of a profitable corset factory with a 'nice little park and gardens'. Progressive thinking is articulated by the manic inventor Sir Timothy Strawbridge and his beautiful daughter, who live in a pristine *art deco* house (admittedly with a butler). Sir Timothy wears short-sleeved shirts and pioneers a succession of labour-saving devices, culminating in the 'Strawbridge Miracle Kitchen', which appears to include early versions of both the microwave oven and the dishwasher.

Unlike the councillors, Gribble and his friends are pure and good. He takes out a crippling loan in order to feed his landlady and her numerous children. As for Sir Timothy, he courteously invites an itinerant busker to join him in his house for refreshment, and encourages an improbable inter-class love affair between Gribble and his daughter, whom he leaves alone in the garden, hoping that they will be 'moonstruck'. The Strawbridges also urge Gribble to stand himself for the council, despite his own reservations. 'A chap like me couldn't be a councillor,' he says. 'I haven't the brains to be a politician.'

The Strawbridges thus anticipate the breaking down of class barriers that, with mass approval, was confidently predicted to be an outcome of the war. According to a prescient George Orwell, whose essay 'The Lion and the Unicorn' was published in February 1941, the process had already begun. 'In 1910,' he observed, 'every human being in these islands could be "placed" in an instant by his clothes, manners and accent. That is no longer the case.' After 1918, there had begun to appear 'something that had never existed in England before: people of indeterminate social class'. Modern industrial methods demanded 'less muscular effort', with the old-style 'proletarian' predominating only in the heavy-industry areas of the North. No longer crippled by exhaustion after their day's work, the beneficiaries of a free education and with access to free libraries, workers were able to read the same books, watch the same films and listen to the same radio programmes as the rich. The differences in their way of life had been further diminished by 'the mass-production of cheap clothes and improvements in housing'. There were still slums, 'a blot on civilization, but much building has been done during the past ten years, largely by the local authorities. The modern council house, with its bathroom and electric light, is smaller than the stockbroker's villa, but it is recognisably the same kind of house, which the farm labourer's cottage is not. A person who has grown up in a council housing estate is likely to be - indeed, visibly *is* - more middle class in outlook than a person who has grown up in a slum.'

The Strawbridges, standing for modernity, progress and, implicitly, socialism, believe with Orwell that the provision of decent housing is a responsibility of the state. It soon transpires that Miss Strawbridge, a schoolteacher on her summer holidays, is also a student of architecture and town-planning and is herself the author of the Tangleton 'Re-development Plan'. Gribble asks what this means. 'Making a beautiful town out of a jerry-built left-over of the Industrial Revolution,' she replies. 'It's making decent homes for decent people to live in. It'll mean tearing down everything that's dirty and ugly and building up something clean and fresh. Everyone getting together and working to a plan, instead of just muddling along, each one thinking only of his own interest.' If class privileges were perpetuated by the very fabric of Britain - Orwell yearned for a time when 'the country houses will be turned into children's holiday camps' - modern, council-owned developments were surely the answer.

'The place to look for the germs of the future England,' Orwell continued, 'is in light-industry areas and along the arterial roads. In Slough, Dagenham, Barnet, Letchworth, Hayes - everywhere, indeed, on the outskirts of great towns - the old pattern is gradually changing into something new. In these vast new wildernesses of glass and brick the sharp distinctions of the older kind of town, with its slums and mansions, or of the country, with its manor-houses and squalid cottages, no longer exist. There are wide gradations of income, but it is the same kind of life that is being lived at different levels, in labour-saving flats or council houses, along the concrete roads and in the naked democracy of the swimming pools. It is a rather restless, cultureless life, centring round tinned food, *Picture Post,* the radio and the internal combustion engine. It is a civilization in which children grow up with an intimate knowledge of magnetoes and in complete ignorance of the Bible. To that civilization belong the people who are most at home and most definitely *of* the modern world, the technicians and the higher-paid skilled workers, the airmen and their mechanics, the radio experts, film producers, popular journalists and industrial chemists. They are the indeterminate stratum at which the older class distinctions are beginning to break down.'

The urge to sweep away what was dirty and ugly and class-ridden is sufficient to explain the carelessness with which historic buildings were treated after the war, and the enthusiasm for re-developing, rather than re-constructing, our shattered town centres. 'Modernist' architecture, the dominant style of the mid-20th century, seemed to offer the 'clean and fresh' alternatives that were advocated by Miss Strawbridge in *Snoops*. In Powell and Pressburger's classic film *A Matter of Life and Death,* released in December 1946, the architecture of 'the other world' - presumably Heaven itself - is clearly the work of a modernist. Functional, unornamented buildings - the machine aesthetic - were the modernists' stock in trade. The reality tended to be disappointing, as concrete is notorious for not weathering well. In the post-war period, unadorned, often brutally functional concrete buildings - flat-roofed shops and office blocks, multi-storey car parks, council flats and the main post office in almost every town - became part of the national landscape, on which they are commonly regarded as a blight. Even the Duke of Westminster was beguiled, unleashing a modernist architect on his family seat in Cheshire. (The result, a white, flat-roofed eyesore of the 1970s, has since been 'de-modernised' and now resembles a French *château*.)

An ancient market-town which, like Tangleton, could easily have been mistaken for a 'jerry-built left-over of the Industrial Revolution', Basingstoke had grown rapidly since the Great War, its population of 5,800 in 1921 rising to around 16,000 in 1941. Where once they were employed in trade or agriculture, the men of Basingstoke found work mostly on the railways or in engineering and metal-working, either at Thornycroft's factory in fields to the west of the town or at the Wallis and Steevens foundry on Station Hill. Women not in domestic service were chiefly engaged in the production of clothing and textiles, for Burberry's, Mares or Gerrish, Ames and Simpkins. Meanwhile, in a wheat field on the Kingsclere Road, Eli Lilly had in 1939 completed their stylish, brilliant-white, six-storey pharmaceutical plant, a striking landmark (albeit camouflaged during the war) that was a sign of things to come. It was staffed, no doubt, by industrial chemists of indeterminate class.

There was a local bus service at last, established by the Venture Bus Company in 1926, and a southern bypass, begun in 1929 and completed in 1932. The Electric Cinema in Lower Wote Street had, since 1910, offered an alternative form of entertainment to the traditional drunken night in the pub. The national and multi-national chain stores had already invaded the High Street, undermining its individuality. Branches of Woolworth's and Boot's had appeared at the London Street end, in 1921 and 1929 respectively. In 1934 they were joined by W.H. Smith in the Market Place and by Marks and Spencer in Winchester Street, with Montague Burton's purveying their famous brand of cheap, natty suiting from a shop that was erected there in 1938. An increasingly homogeneous Basingstoke, on the junction of several arterial roads, was already developing into a listless 'light-industry area' of the kind identified by Orwell, though the workers in these various industries continued to live in depressing terraced houses like those in Lower Brook Street.

Lack of planning and investment in the real-life Tangleton had been a cause for concern as early as 1933, when a committee made up of representatives from Basingstoke Borough Council, the Chamber of Commerce, local Rotarians and members of the Trades and Labour Council had published a promotional brochure, hopefully entitled 'Bring your Factories to Basingstoke'. Re-development became a pressing priority in the years to 1961, when the population of the town rose to 25,940. However, Miss Strawbridge need not have worried. At the very time that *Snoops* was in production, Professor (later Sir) Patrick Abercrombie was putting the finishing touches to his *Greater London Plan*.

Abercrombie had been commissioned by the Minister of Works and Buildings (shades of the 'Minister of Municipal Research and Reconstruction' in the film) to consider the future of London, which since 1940 had been steadily wrecked by German bombing, and even now was subject to terrifying attacks by 'doodlebugs'. His brief was to prepare a post-war strategy for housing, transport and industry in the capital, which, it was feared, was over-populated, under-resourced, and no longer viable.

It was Abercrombie's radical idea to shift a total of 1,033,000 Londoners into 'New Towns' that would be created in the Home Counties, around small villages like Harlow and Stevenage. The population of each 'New Town' would be limited to 60,000 inhabitants. Others would be dispersed to existing towns such as Ashford in Kent, Chelmsford and Witham in Essex, Aylesbury and Bletchley in Buckinghamshire and, of course, Basingstoke, where there was ample room for expansion.

An architect in the tradition of Ebenezer Howard (pioneer in 1898 of the 'Garden City') and Le Corbusier (who believed in the 'Green City' and saw housing as 'a branch of the public services'), Abercrombie envisaged 'standards of open space' for his brave new world, along with networks of 'parkways' and a 'Green Belt' which was to be kept free from building development. Miss Strawbridge's 'nice little park and gardens' would have met with his wholehearted approval. The audacity of Abercrombie's plan is breathtaking. Even more remarkable is the fact that it has been largely realised.

The architects of the London County Council, Abercrombie's disciples and collaborators, included such politically-motivated idealists as Graeme Shankland. A branch secretary of the Communist Party of Great Britain, whose homosexual love-life was carefully monitored by MI5, Shankland was the man who, in 1951, came up with a futuristic design for the bomb-wrecked Elephant and Castle. In 1959, he submitted plans for an Abercrombian 'New Town' at Hook, a tiny staging post on the A30, east of Basingstoke. Its central facilities were to be grouped in a vast 'Megastructure', which was to be on a raised deck above the main road. The Megastructure was to be connected to the satellite housing estates by a series of pedestrian walkways, prototypes of those at the Southbank Centre in Lambeth, which

Shankland was to help design in the 1960s. The guiding principle was to place people and cars on separate levels, so that neither should impede the other. There would be no need for traffic lights, and no need ever to cross a road.

Endorsed by both Hampshire County Council and the Ministry of Housing, Shankland's alarming vision for Hook was never to be realised. Discussions had barely begun when, it is said, word reached the team from the Prime Minister, Harold Macmillan: the proposed new bus station appeared to be on a site favoured by the Queen's uncle (possibly David Bowes-Lyon) for birdwatching. The Greater London Council was, in any case, refused planning permission in 1962. It was not discouraged from publishing its illustrated scheme for Hook, *The Planning of a New Town,* in 1965, a work of far-reaching influence on urban design, or from assessing Basingstoke, Andover and Tadley for possible expansion. Each of these towns would now have to take a share of the 100,000 people that had been intended for Hook.

Far from being opposed to expansion on such a scale, Basingstoke Borough Council approved a transformation that was more likely to further their vested interests than to thwart them. The various authorities agreed to a joint plan in the summer of 1960, whereby Basingstoke would receive an additional 40,000 inhabitants, and release vast acreages of the surrounding farmland for development. The requirement was for 11,500 new homes by 1976. The old 'Top of Town' shopping centre was deemed to be inadequate, so a new one was planned in the valley. Unsurprisingly, a blueprint was found in the shelved plans for Hook. Over seven weeks, some 15,000 people attended an exhibition of the proposals in the Town Hall. Astonishingly, there were only 273 objections. Even allowing for their recent dilution by incomers, the townspeople were apparently unconcerned that 146 acres of the historic town centre had been designated a 'Comprehensive Development Area', a euphemism disguising the fact that it was to be totally demolished. In August 1962, as the plans were unveiled, a headline in a special supplement to the *Hants and Berks Gazette* captured the air of excitement and optimism: 'South's first town of the motor-car age. Shopping centre on a platform. Separate routes for cars and pedestrians. The showpiece town of the South of England. That will be the Basingstoke of the 1980s.'

'Alas! Poor Basingstoke, no one seems to mind very much,' said a bemused John Arlott. The dramatic process of demolition, which began in 1965, was nevertheless sobering for onlookers. According to one incomer, Mrs Davey, happy to have escaped the grime and poverty of her native London, 'tears were silently shed' as it rapidly turned 'my new Hampshire haven into an endless dusty hell'. Ian Hayes, then a young reporter on the *Gazette*, recalls 'the dancing flames of the demolition men's bonfires on dark winter afternoons. The entire bottom of the town was shut off behind hoardings and there was rubble, dust and mud everywhere. Most dramatic was a bird's eye view while flying over the town in a helicopter from R.A.F. Odiham, showing the whole expanse of bare white chalk on the re-development site. It looked as if a giant hand had scooped out the centre of the town leaving just the fringes.' These operations were destructive not only of Basingstoke's oldest buildings and of its former means of sustenance - the Gerrish, Ames and Simpkins and Wallis and Steevens factories were demolished, along with the Cattle Market - but also of its character. 'It was not a place of great beauty or architectural merit, but it was big enough to be interesting and small enough for people to know each other and have a sense of belonging, both to the town and the countryside … Set in superb farming country it was as typically Hampshire as fresh watercress, early strawberries, Alton ales and the sound of a John Arlott commentary on a sleepy summer's day.'

Basingstoke's new 'shopping centre on a platform' includes 'The Walks', completed in 1971, and 'The Malls', built between 1978 and 1981. For the sake of such ill-conceived ventures, numerous hapless tradesmen and residents had to be evicted from their properties, many of which were left as cleared sites for years. Alfie Cole felt that he was to be inadequately compensated for his stables on Basing Road. With the help of a former Fleet Street journalist, Charles Hemsley, a campaign was whipped up in the press. Cole's stunts included driving to Downing Street in a pony and trap in 1966 to petition Harold Wilson, and 'dumping lorry loads of top soil at strategic parts of the town during the morning rush hour'. Eventually, a satisfactory sum was forthcoming, and Cole retreated to the countryside.

A more poignant tale was that of Mr A.M. Oliver and his 81-year-old mother, whose family had lived at 9 New Road since it was first built in the 1870s. A horseshoe hung beside the front door to bring good luck. 'Mother and I don't want to leave,' said Mr Oliver. 'This has been our home for 52 years and my grandmother's before me. We have had some good times here in the old days and the thought of it being pulled down is very distressing.' His mother seemed resigned to her fate. 'I would like one of the old people's bungalows in Church Square,' she said. 'If not we shall have to accept whatever is offered to us.'

The insensitive, even contemptuous attitude of the planners towards the people of Basingstoke was gradually revealed. Money being tight, much of the scheme had to be abandoned or re-written. The 'Ringway', opened in 1971, was not the fast channel for traffic that had been intended. Much of it was to remain single-carriageway for years and most of the promised bridges and underpasses are unbuilt to this day. To their consternation, users of the West Ham Swimming Baths found the encircling Ringway an impenetrable barrier. The open-air pool, built in 1906, was a much-loved civic amenity, despite being famous for its icy water. When there was no way of getting to it across a dangerous road, it simply fell into disuse, a cause of bitter resentment among the locals.

It was clear also that much of town-centre demolition had been premature and unnecessary. Plans for a vast 'civic centre' between Cross Street and Church Square were shelved, but not before this historic and picturesque area of the town had been completely flattened. The losses included nos.47/49 Church Street (latterly the Army and Navy Stores), the last survivor in a row of jettied shops (others had been re-developed in 1937) that was at least 400 years old. The few surviving buildings of this age in Church Street and Cross Street bear witness to the loss. Pointless open spaces mark the sites of those that were quite needlessly sacrificed.

The bold experiment that was the cause of such distress was acknowledged by 1976 to have been a failure. The removal of much of its workforce had failed to improve the situation in London. Despite Abercrombie's forecast, there had been no 'urban renewal'. The Greater London Council (successor to the London County Council) terminated its arrangement with Basingstoke in December 1977, and gave up altogether on 'New' and 'Expanded' towns. To quote the *Gazette,* the town had been transformed into 'a mini metropolis of light industry and ex-Londoners'. They had had their pick of new council accommodation in either Basingstoke or Andover and plentiful offers of work, with newly-arrived firms such as Lansing Bagnell and Van Moppes and at the Atomic Weapons Research Establishment in Aldermaston. Once they had found their feet and grown used to the jibes of the 'carrot-crunchers' or 'swede-bashers' - their names for the indigenous population - the 'Cockney scum' reaped the benefits of living in an increasingly prosperous town, which now has some of the highest rates of pay and of full-time employment in the country. It appears, however, to be a rather restless, cultureless life, centring on ready-meals, *Hello!* magazine, satellite T.V. and the internal combustion engine.

The growth of Basingstoke has since been relentless - the Labour government of Gordon Brown imposed a target of 945 new homes per year - but its reputation is hardly as 'the showpiece town of the South'. Outlying farms and settlements continue to be swallowed up by vast housing estates. The earliest of these are notorious for their poor design. At Winklebury, the community school was crassly built on top of an iron-age fort. At Popley and Brighton Hill, intimidating gangs of youths gather in the subways. The social housing at Oakridge, including Basingstoke's only residential tower block, the 13-storey Oakridge Tower, had become so hard to let by the 1990s that much of it had to be demolished. Each of these self-contained suburbs is connected by the 'Ringway' and a dreary network of dual carriageways and roundabouts, including that at Brighton Hill, which has been listed among the top ten worst roundabouts in the country. The landscape is so monotonous that only the roundabouts stand out. As for 'The Malls', it was ranked in a survey in 1999 among the 200 worst retail centres in the country.

'Modernist' architecture has failed less spectacularly in Basingstoke than in the 'New Towns' that were built from scratch - horrors like Bracknell, with its utterly dispiriting town centre. Cumbernauld in Scotland is the latest and most complete example of a New Town. Intended for Glaswegian 'overspill', it has been ludicrously compared to a 'hilltop town out of Italy'. At Cumbernauld, the idea of a 'Megastructure' was taken up with enthusiasm by the presiding architect, Geoffrey Copcutt. The result - lauded by his colleagues - is a soulless, concrete carbuncle, so grim that it has been painted white in an attempt to cheer it up. In the Channel 4 series *Demolition,* broadcast in December 2005, it was voted 'the worst building in Britain'. Cumbernauld's indoor shopping 'mall' - Britain's first - has been deserted by the major retailers, and the pedestrian walkways are hostile, sinister wind tunnels. The whole place is a wilderness of tower blocks and roundabouts. Hook and all Hampshire should be thankful to the Queen and her birdwatching uncle for sparing them from such a fate.

The unfortunate residents of Peterlee New Town in County Durham, a dense forest of tower blocks, have had Victor Pasmore's 'Apollo Pavilion' foisted on them - a jumble of concrete blocks, 82 feet wide, that is half sculpture, half bridge - though it is almost universally reviled (they refer to it as 'the Montrosity'), and the steps that gave it some functional value have had to be removed, to deter vandals. It is powerfully symbolic of the gulf between the self-congratulatory, middle-class, left-wing intellectuals of the architectural schools and the 'little people' whose interests they claimed to serve and who, in the post-war period, ill-advisedly reposed such trust in them.

# VI. Even at Ulubrae

The re-development of Basingstoke's historic heart was a catastrophe from which it will never fully recover. It is a tragic injustice that its finest buildings should have been dispensed with by politically motivated Londoners (the architects of the L.C.C.), in the interest not of its existing population but of the London 'overspill'. Bedford House, Queen Anne House and the striking Wesleyan Chapel in Church Street were three of the most notable casualties, all sacrificed in the cause of the 'Great Wall of Basingstoke'. If that excrescence had only been set back a few yards, those buildings could have been preserved, but this would never have suited the planners.

Admittedly, the area had become very shabby and run-down - like post-war Britain generally. Aunt Peggy's garden had been sold off as a nursery and was full of abandoned glasshouses. Yet her former home was historically and architecturally significant. When it was being dismantled in 1966, the Willis Museum recovered from a passageway, where they had been concealed behind green stippled wallpaper that might have been Peggy's, fragments of the original, late 17th-century Spanish leather wall-hangings. Painted in scarlet, gilded and, finally, embossed with designs of birds and foliage scrolls, these were incredibly rare. Today, Queen Anne House would be a highly desirable property. With such buildings at its heart, Basingstoke had all the charm and individuality of a Farnham or a Wallingford, the potential to thrive without the necessity for a holocaust. It needed investment, and a certain amount of sympathetic development. It did not need to have its heart cut out.

One is surprised and grateful that so much has survived, especially at the 'Top of Town', including all but one of the great coaching inns. The exception is the picturesque but blighted Angel. Burberry lived to witness its reincarnation as the branch of Barclays bank that it has remained ever since. A cash dispenser marks the exact site of the archway bench where local shopkeepers, pot of ale in hand, once idled away their time. I believe the former Maidenhead Inn to be the building next door, now much reduced in status - there are betting and charity shops on the ground floor - and heavily disguised under later accretions. It cries out for the attention of an architectural historian, to confirm or disprove my theory. The Maidenhead was, of course, the building where Katherine of Aragon lodged for a night in 1501.

The modernised centre of Basingstoke has seemed considerably less depressing since the opening, in 2002, of Festival Place, which straddles what used to be Aunt Peggy's garden. It is, however, an unabashed shrine to consumerism, tending only to reinforce the view that Basingstoke is rampantly philistine. It may be the nation's favourite pastime, but there must be more to life than shopping! Basingstoke needs a wealthy benefactor like Diogenes of Oinoanda (in modern Turkey), who in the 2$^{nd}$ century A.D., as a corrective to the greed and consumerism of his neighbours, built a rectangular piazza in the middle of town. On the walls of the surrounding, 80-metre portico, Diogenes had carved, for the edification of the townsfolk, a dense, 25,000-word statement of the teachings of Epicurus. If only a modern-day Diogenes would step forward (perhaps Lord Sainsbury or Lord Lloyd-Webber), and a site were made available at some particularly desolate spot, such as 'The Malls', the people of Basingstoke might also benefit from Epicurean wisdom:

*'Luxurious foods and drink ... in no way produce freedom from harm and a healthy condition in the flesh.'*

*'One must regard wealth beyond what is natural as of no more use than water to a container that is full to overflowing.'*

*'Real value is generated not by theatres and baths and perfumes and ointments ... but by natural science.'*

Like the beneficent Diogenes, I would suggest the raising in appropriate locations in Basingstoke of four dignified statues, based on descriptions and surviving portraits and inscribed as follows:

*Walter de Merton, a proud son of Basingstoke, Bishop of Rochester and Chancellor of England, founder in 1264 of Merton College, Oxford. Intended for the benefit of his numerous kindred, it was the first self-governing university college in England, and the model for all that have followed. The family farm, which Walter left to the college, was under your feet. Descendants of his eight sisters are probably all around you.*

*Remember Jane Austen (1775 - 1817), who shopped here before you. She spent her early years at Steventon, and came to Basingstoke for all necessary purchases. John Ring of Church Street supplied her bed and the portable writing-desk on which she wrote her great novels. These were intended to amuse her family, but have since delighted the whole world. She describes assemblies like those she attended at Basingstoke, where once she danced twenty dances in an evening without any fatigue. When on her travels, she changed coaches here.* Sic parvis magna.

*Honour the memory of Thomas Burberry (1835 - 1926), a true Christian. From his draper's shop in Winchester Street, he effected a revolution in fashion. His famous 'gabardine' cloth was inspired by the peasant smock, such as was commonly worn in this town. He designed the first raincoats, which came to be considered the height of glamour. The peak of Everest, the South Pole, the skies above the Atlantic - each was conquered with the help of Burberry clothes. He was a great friend and benefactor to Basingstoke.*

*Here lived Margaret Chandler (1822 - 1915), after whom Margaret River, in Western Australia, is named. She was the eldest of the six beautiful daughters of James Whicher, Surgeon of Petersfield, known as 'the Bewitchers'. Her cousin John Garrett Bussell, who hoped to marry her, discovered the river and named it in her honour,* anno *1839. Margaret was married in turn to Joseph Shebbeare and Samuel Chandler, Attorneys of Basingstoke, and lived at Queen Anne House in Church Street, 1852 - 1901. She led a life of blameless obscurity and quiet self-sacrifice. The Margaret River region is famous today for its golden beaches, surfing, whale-watching and vineyards.*

Finally, Diogenes would surely have approved of Horace's lines about the futility of travel, and would have wanted them to be inscribed near a travel agency:

*caelum, non animum, mutant qui trans mare currunt.*
*strenua nos exercet inertia: navibus atque*
*quadrigis petimus bene vivere, quod petis hic est,*
*est Ulubris, animus si te non deficit aequus.*

Some thirty miles from Rome, on the way to the Pontine Marshes, Ulubrae was proverbial among classical authors for its dullness. Horace wisely advocates coming to terms with Ulubrae, if one has to live or spend time there, just as one should with Basingstoke:

*There might be better weather overseas, but the same old you comes home.*
*Why all this pointless rushing about, thinking we are living it up*
*in our planes and cars? What you seek is here -*
*yes, even at Basingstoke. It's your frame of mind that counts.*

*Katherine of Aragon slept here? The supposed Kingsmill House,*
*later the Maidenhead Inn, now much reduced in status.*

# Manuscript Sources

The following have been of particular value: in the Hampshire Archives, the Basingstoke Tithe Map and Apportionment 1841 (21 M65/F7/13/1-2); Kingsmill family papers (19 M61); John Ring's ledgers (8 M62/12-15); letter appealing for donations in aid of Mrs Martin (44 M69/M3/4/9); constables returns 1671, with the earliest reference to the Maidenhead Inn (44 M69/G4/1/133); will of John Lyford (148 M71/4/18/47); will of John Ring senior (8 M62/65); administration of Ann Ring (21 M65/D4/1788/40); Curtis deeds (10 M57/C39 and 67/M83/10; Davies deeds (11 M49/E/T61-73); abstracts of Mrs Margaret Chandler's title to various properties (63 M83/B1/3-33); wills of Joseph Shebbeare (5 M62/3/page 451) and James Whicher (5 M62/15/page 27); in the Willis Museum, Basingstoke, various newspaper cuttings and manuscripts, such as a transcript of George Woodman's diary entry describing the celebrations on the wedding day of the Prince and Princess of Wales; V. Fenwick Bedford's letter to George Willis dated 30 April 1958; typescripts headed *Thomas Burberry, 1835 - 1926, Burberry History  Est. 1856, Homes of the Burberry Family* and *The Great Fire of Basingstoke*, along with Ian Hayes, *A Memory of Basingstoke in the 1960s;* in the Basingstoke Library, a valuable collection of cuttings and old photographs, including some of Queen Anne House; in the J.S. Battye Library of Western Australian History in the State Library of Western Australia, Perth, the voluminous Bussell collection, including particularly James Whicher's letters to John Garrett Bussell between May and October 1838 (MN586/337A/422-4, 426-7 and 429); in the Probate Registry, Margaret Chandler's will, proved in 1915; in the National Archives, the wills of Thomas Weir, 1799, Edward Vernon Yates, 1801, and Thomas Legal Yates, 1835; there is also a Tauke/Fisher pedigree (Pedigree Add MSS 1552 1573). George H.C. Whicher's *Whicher Memoirs,* a copy of which is in my possession, afford the closest glimpses we are ever likely to get of Margaret Chandler.

# Select Bibliography

Barbara Applin, *Roundabout Basingstoke* (Basingstoke, 1999).

Arthur Attwood, 'A Farm Stood in the Heart of Basingstoke', *Basingstoke Gazette*, 15 August 1980.

Arthur Attwood, 'A Fine Gentleman' [James Lunn], *Basingstoke Gazette*, 6 June 1986.

Arthur Attwood, *St Michael's Church, Basingstoke: A Short History* (Basingstoke, 1995).

Arthur Attwood, 'Samuel Attwood's Diary', *Basingstoke Gazette,* 30 October 1981.

*Jane Austen's Letters,* ed. Deirdre Le Faye (Oxford, 1996).

F.W. Baigent and J.E. Millard, *A History of the Ancient Town and Manor of Basingstoke* (London, 1889).

*Calendar of Charters and Documents relating to Selborne and its Priory,* ed. W. Dunn Macray, 2 vols. (Winchester, 1891-4).

'Cheltenham Ladies and the Chavs', *The Daily Telegraph,* 14 December 2004.

Edward Copeland, *'Persuasion:* The Jane Austen Consumer's Guide', *Persuasions* (Journal of the Jane Austen Society of North America), Vol.15 (1993).

Diogenes of Oinoanda, *The Epicurean Inscription,* trans. Martin Ferguson Smith (Naples, 1993).

'Fashion Crimes', *The Sun,* 23 January 2009.

Mary Felgate and Barbara Applin, *Going Down Church Street to the Felgate Bookshop* (Basingstoke, 1998).

'When Formby Came to Film', *Basingstoke Gazette,* 2 April 2004.

Michael Franks, *The Clerk of Basingstoke: A Life of Walter de Merton* (Oxford, 2003).

David French and Janet Firth, *Barkham - A History* (Barkham, 2000).

Arthur Hailstones, 'Looking Back - I Remember', Parts I and II, *Hants and Berks Gazette,* March 1938

*Hampshire Archaeology and Local History Newsletter,* Vol.I, No.6 (November 1967).

*Hants Directory 1784.*

Florence Emily Hardy, *The Later Years of Thomas Hardy, 1892 - 1928* (London, 1930).

*The Collected Letters of Thomas Hardy,* II, ed. Richard Little Purdy and Michael Millgate (Oxford, 1980).

Owen Hatherley, 'A New Career in Town', www.pd.org/Perforations/perf29/Oh1.pdf

Anne Hawker, *The Story of Basingstoke* (Basingstoke, 1999).

Anne Hawker, *Voices of Basingstoke, 1400 - 1600* (Basingstoke, 1983).

*High Street, Petersfield* (Petersfield Area Historical Society, 1984).

*Kelly's Directory 1867* and *1898*.

Deirdre Le Faye, *Jane Austen's Steventon* (Chawton, 2007).

Deirdre Le Faye, *Jane Austen: The World of her Novels* (London, 2002).

Mary Oliver, *Church Cottage, Basingstoke: Historical Notes* (Basingstoke, 2007).

George Orwell, 'The Lion and the Unicorn', in Sonia Orwell and Ian Angus eds., *The Collected Essays, Journalism and Letters of George Orwell,* II (London, 1968).

*Matthew Paris's English History,* trans. J.A. Giles, II (London, 1853).

Malcolm Parker: *Images of England: Basingstoke* (Stroud, 2009).

Arthur W. Saunders, 'Basingstoke in the 19th Century', Parts I - IV, *Hants and Berks Gazette,* July 1939.

'A Sexagenarian' [James Edward Austen-Leigh], *Recollections of the Early Days of the Vine Hunt* (privately printed, 1865).

G.D. Squibb, *Founder's Kin: Privilege and Pedigree* (Oxford, 1972).

Diana Stanley, *Within Living Memory* (Bournemouth, 1967).

David Starkey, *Henry - Virtuous Prince* (London, 2008).

Eric Stokes, *The Making of Basingstoke from Prehistory to the Present Day,* ed. Bob and Barbara Applin (Basingstoke, 2008).

Eric Stokes, *The Things They Say About Basingstoke* (revised edition, Fareham, 1997).

Edward Shann, *Cattle Chosen: The Story of the First Group Settlement in Western Australia, 1829 - 1841* (Oxford, 1926).

Claire Tomalin, *Jane Austen: A Life* (London, 1997).

*Un Principe di Toscana in Inghilterra e in Irlanda nel 1669,* ed. Anna Maria Crino (Rome, 1968).

Robin Vick, 'The Basingstoke Assemblies', *The Collected Reports of the Jane Austen Society ,* LV.

*The Victoria County History of Hampshire,* ed. W. Page, IV (London, 1911).

*Visitor's Guide to Old Basingstoke* (Friends of the Willis Museum, no date).

A.R. Wagner, *Pedigree and Progress: Essays in the Genealogical Interpretation of History* (London, 1975).

*The Correspondence of Thomas Warton,* ed. David Farrier (Atlanta, 1995).

Gilbert White, *The Natural History and Antiquities of Selborne,* ed. Thomas Bell, 2 vols. (London, 1877).

William White, *Directory of Hants 1859*.

Rupert Willoughby, *Sherborne St John and The Vyne in the Time of Jane Austen* (Sherborne St John, 2002).

George Woodman, 'Reminiscences of Basingstoke - 70 to 100 Years Ago', *Hants and Berks Gazette,* Parts I and II, March 1926.

'Peter Youngman' (obituary), *The Independent,* 10 June 2005.

# Index

Festival Place, 58, 94.
Fisher family, 32-3.
FitzAce family, 25.
FitzOliver, Walter, 25.
Fleurs-de-Lys Inn, 53.
Formby, George, 80 *et seq.*
'Gabardine', 13.
George Hotel, 42.
Gerrish, Ames and Simpkins, 14, 86, 89.
Goldings Park, 20, 50, 59.
Grahame-White, Claude, 16.
Grosseteste, Robert, Bishop of Lincoln, 27-8.
Hackett, General Sir John, 76.
　Sir Winthrop, 76.
Hackwood Park, 57, 61.
　Road, 14, 20.
Hardy, Thomas, 10.
Hayward, Sophy, 70.
Heppingstone, Ellen, 75.
Herriard, Richard de, 25.
High Street, 41, 49, 53, 58.
Hook, 17, 87-9.
Horace, 96.
Hospital of St John, 29, 33.
Isaacs, Sam, 76.
John of Basingstoke, 26-7.
Joice's Yard, 42.
Katherine of Aragon, 34-5.
Kingsmill family, 34 *et seq.,* 41-2, 53.
Lanham, Edgar, 14.
Little Lane, 58, 62.
Lloyd-Webber, Andrew, the Lord, 36, 94.
London Street, 42, 53.
Lyford family, 39, 40, 42n., 46, 47.

Lucy, Philip de, 26, 28.
McDonald's Restaurant, 22, 34, 53.
Magalotti, Count Lorenzo, 10.
Maidenhead Inn, 10, 42-4, 50, 53, 93-4.
Mallory and Irvine, 17.
Malls, The, 14, 89, 94.
Mares, John, 14, 86.
Margaret River, 74-5, 79, 96.
Market Place, 18, 22, 41, 44, 49, 54, 55, 58.
Martin, Mrs Mary, 43, 45, 50, 51.
May family, 42, 62.
　Brewery, 56, 61.
'Megastructures', 87.
Merton Farm, 56-7, 60.
　Priory, 25, 27.
Michaelmas Fair, 60.
Molloy, Capt. John and Georgiana, 65, 67, 69, 70.
Montfort, Simon de, Earl of Leicester, 27, 30.
New Street, 12, 14, 57, 58.
New Towns, 87 *et seq.*
North Hants Ironworks, 55.
Odiham, 62, 89.
Oliver, Walter, 32.
Orwell, George, 83-6.
Paulet family, 36, 42, 44, 46, 57.
Peskett family, 78-9.
Petersfield, 66-7, 71, 77.
Portsmouth family, 33, 56-7, 60.
Potter's Lane, 58.
Queen Anne House, 63, 82, 93, 96.
Railways, coming of the, 54-5, 78.
Red Lion Inn, 42-3.
Reeve house, 62, 82.
Rider, Mr and Mrs, 49, 50, 51.

*No.12 High Street, Petersfield, the birthplace in 1822 of Margaret Whicher*

By the same author …

## CHAWTON: JANE AUSTEN'S VILLAGE

'An excellent example of how a village guide can and should be written and produced'
*The Coat of Arms*

## SELBORNE: GILBERT WHITE'S VILLAGE

'A real treat … it brilliantly conveys a sense of Selborne's development from the Middle Ages to the present day … Well-written and beautifully produced, this is an example of local history at its best'
Mark Page, *Hampshire Field Club and Archaeological Society Newsletter*

'This hugely enjoyable treatise, greatly enhanced by the fine delicate drawings of Julie Anne Hudson, with its easy style and wonderfully researched detail is a real pleasure to read'
Julie Edwards, *The Selborne Association Newsletter*

## SHERBORNE ST JOHN AND THE VYNE
## IN THE TIME OF JANE AUSTEN

'Remarkably concise and informative'
David Selwyn, *The Jane Austen Society Newsletter*

# A KEY TO ODIHAM CASTLE

'The author draws upon both written and archaeological evidence to conjure up the medieval appearance and atmosphere of the castle'
   *Hampshire Chronicle*

Forthcoming …

## THE INCREDIBLE JOURNEY OF VICTOR HUGO'S DOG

(a true-life romance set in *fin-de-siècle* France, Switzerland and England)

RUPERT WILLOUGHBY is a prize-winning historian who specialises in the domestic and social life of the past. A graduate with First Class Honours in History from the University of London, he is the author of the best-selling *Life in Medieval England* for Pitkin, of guides to castles owned by English Heritage and Hampshire County Council, and of a series of popular histories of places, including *Chawton: Jane Austen's Village, Selborne: Gilbert White's Village* and *Sherborne St John and the Vyne in the Time of Jane Austen*. His most recent book, *Reading and its Contribution to World Culture,* is an antidote to the vulgarity of modern Reading.

He has published numerous articles, contributes regular obituaries to *The Daily Telegraph,* writes histories of houses, occasionally broadcasts to the nation and is an experienced lecturer, whose repertoire ranges from the life and personalities of the Middle Ages to the world of Jane Austen.